GNU Libtool Reference Manual

A catalogue record for this book is available from the Hong Kong Public Libraries.

Published in Hong Kong by Samurai Media Limited.

Email: info@samuraimedia.org

ISBN 978-988-8381-48-7

Background Cover Image by https://www.flickr.com/people/webtreatsetc/

Table of Contents

1 Introduction

In the past, if you were a source code package developer and wanted to take advantage of the power of shared libraries, you needed to write custom support code for each platform on which your package ran. You also had to design a configuration interface so that the package installer could choose what sort of libraries were built.

GNU Libtool simplifies your job by encapsulating both the platform-specific dependencies, and the user interface, in a single script. GNU Libtool is designed so that the complete functionality of each host type is available via a generic interface, but nasty quirks are hidden from the programmer.

GNU Libtool's consistent interface is reassuring... users don't need to read obscure documentation to have their favorite source package build shared libraries. They just run your package `configure` script (or equivalent), and libtool does all the dirty work.

There are several examples throughout this document. All assume the same environment: we want to build a library, `libhello`, in a generic way.

`libhello` could be a shared library, a static library, or both... whatever is available on the host system, as long as libtool has been ported to it.

This chapter explains the original design philosophy of libtool. Feel free to skip to the next chapter, unless you are interested in history, or want to write code to extend libtool in a consistent way.

1.1 Motivation for writing libtool

Since early 1995, several different GNU developers have recognized the importance of having shared library support for their packages. The primary motivation for such a change is to encourage modularity and reuse of code (both conceptually and physically) in GNU programs.

Such a demand means that the way libraries are built in GNU packages needs to be general, to allow for any library type the package installer might want. The problem is compounded by the absence of a standard procedure for creating shared libraries on different platforms.

The following sections outline the major issues facing shared library support in GNU, and how shared library support could be standardized with libtool.

The following specifications were used in developing and evaluating this system:

1. The system must be as elegant as possible.
2. The system must be fully integrated with the GNU Autoconf and Automake utilities, so that it will be easy for GNU maintainers to use. However, the system must not require these tools, so that it can be used by non-GNU packages.
3. Portability to other (non-GNU) architectures and tools is desirable.

1.2 Implementation issues

The following issues need to be addressed in any reusable shared library system, specifically libtool:

1. The package installer should be able to control what sort of libraries are built.

2. It can be tricky to run dynamically linked programs whose libraries have not yet been installed. `LD_LIBRARY_PATH` must be set properly (if it is supported), or programs fail to run.

3. The system must operate consistently even on hosts that don't support shared libraries.

4. The commands required to build shared libraries may differ wildly from host to host. These need to be determined at configure time in a consistent way.

5. It is not always obvious with what prefix or suffix a shared library should be installed. This makes it difficult for `Makefile` rules, since they generally assume that file names are the same from host to host.

6. The system needs a simple library version number abstraction, so that shared libraries can be upgraded in place. The programmer should be informed how to design the interfaces to the library to maximize binary compatibility.

7. The install `Makefile` target should warn the package installer to set the proper environment variables (`LD_LIBRARY_PATH` or equivalent), or run `ldconfig`.

1.3 Other implementations

Even before libtool was developed, many free software packages built and installed their own shared libraries. At first, these packages were examined to avoid reinventing existing features.

Now it is clear that none of these packages have documented the details of shared library systems that libtool requires. So, other packages have been more or less abandoned as influences.

1.4 A postmortem analysis of other implementations

In all fairness, each of the implementations that were examined do the job that they were intended to do, for a number of different host systems. However, none of these solutions seem to function well as a generalized, reusable component.

Most were too complex to use (much less modify) without understanding exactly what the implementation does, and they were generally not documented.

The main difficulty is that different vendors have different views of what libraries are, and none of the packages that were examined seemed to be confident enough to settle on a single paradigm that just *works*.

Ideally, libtool would be a standard that would be implemented as series of extensions and modifications to existing library systems to make them work consistently. However, it is not an easy task to convince operating system developers to mend their evil ways, and people want to build shared libraries right now, even on buggy, broken, confused operating systems.

For this reason, libtool was designed as an independent shell script. It isolates the problems and inconsistencies in library building that plague `Makefile` writers by wrapping the compiler suite on different platforms with a consistent, powerful interface.

With luck, libtool will be useful to and used by the GNU community, and that the lessons that were learned in writing it will be taken up by designers of future library systems.

2 The libtool paradigm

At first, libtool was designed to support an arbitrary number of library object types. After libtool was ported to more platforms, a new paradigm gradually developed for describing the relationship between libraries and programs.

In summary, "libraries are programs with multiple entry points, and more formally defined interfaces."

Version 0.7 of libtool was a complete redesign and rewrite of libtool to reflect this new paradigm. So far, it has proved to be successful: libtool is simpler and more useful than before.

The best way to introduce the libtool paradigm is to contrast it with the paradigm of existing library systems, with examples from each. It is a new way of thinking, so it may take a little time to absorb, but when you understand it, the world becomes simpler.

3 Using libtool

It makes little sense to talk about using libtool in your own packages until you have seen how it makes your life simpler. The examples in this chapter introduce the main features of libtool by comparing the standard library building procedure to libtool's operation on two different platforms:

'a23'   An Ultrix 4.2 platform with only static libraries.

'burger'   A NetBSD/i386 1.2 platform with shared libraries.

You can follow these examples on your own platform, using the preconfigured libtool script that was installed with libtool (see Section 5.4 [Configuring], page 27).

Source files for the following examples are taken from the demo subdirectory of the libtool distribution. Assume that we are building a library, libhello, out of the files foo.c and hello.c.

Note that the foo.c source file uses the cos math library function, which is usually found in the standalone math library, and not the C library (see Section "Trigonometric Functions" in *The GNU C Library Reference Manual*). So, we need to add -lm to the end of the link line whenever we link foo.lo into an executable or a library (see Chapter 9 [Inter-library dependencies], page 47).

The same rule applies whenever you use functions that don't appear in the standard C library... you need to add the appropriate -l*name* flag to the end of the link line when you link against those objects.

After we have built that library, we want to create a program by linking main.o against libhello.

3.1 Creating object files

To create an object file from a source file, the compiler is invoked with the -c flag (and any other desired flags):

```
burger$ gcc -g -O -c main.c
burger$
```

The above compiler command produces an object file, usually named main.o, from the source file main.c.

For most library systems, creating object files that become part of a static library is as simple as creating object files that are linked to form an executable:

```
burger$ gcc -g -O -c foo.c
burger$ gcc -g -O -c hello.c
burger$
```

Shared libraries, however, may only be built from *position-independent code* (PIC). So, special flags must be passed to the compiler to tell it to generate PIC rather than the standard position-dependent code.

Since this is a library implementation detail, libtool hides the complexity of PIC compiler flags and uses separate library object files (the PIC one lives in the .libs subdirectory and the static one lives in the current directory). On systems without shared libraries, the PIC library object files are not created, whereas on systems where all code is PIC, such as AIX, the static ones are not created.

To create library object files for `foo.c` and `hello.c`, simply invoke libtool with the standard compilation command as arguments (see Section 4.1 [Compile mode], page 17):

```
a23$ libtool --mode=compile gcc -g -O -c foo.c
gcc -g -O -c foo.c -o foo.o
a23$ libtool --mode=compile gcc -g -O -c hello.c
gcc -g -O -c hello.c -o hello.o
a23$
```

Note that libtool silently creates an additional control file on each 'compile' invocation. The `.lo` file is the libtool object, which Libtool uses to determine what object file may be built into a shared library. On 'a23', only static libraries are supported so the library objects look like this:

```
# foo.lo - a libtool object file
# Generated by ltmain.sh (GNU libtool) 2.4.6
#
# Please DO NOT delete this file!
# It is necessary for linking the library.

# Name of the PIC object.
pic_object=none

# Name of the non-PIC object.
non_pic_object='foo.o'
```

On shared library systems, libtool automatically generates an additional PIC object by inserting the appropriate PIC generation flags into the compilation command:

```
burger$ libtool --mode=compile gcc -g -O -c foo.c
mkdir .libs
gcc -g -O -c foo.c  -fPIC -DPIC -o .libs/foo.o
gcc -g -O -c foo.c -o foo.o >/dev/null 2>&1
burger$
```

Note that Libtool automatically created `.libs` directory upon its first execution, where PIC library object files will be stored.

Since 'burger' supports shared libraries, and requires PIC objects to build them, Libtool has compiled a PIC object this time, and made a note of it in the libtool object:

```
# foo.lo - a libtool object file
# Generated by ltmain.sh (GNU libtool) 2.4.6
#
# Please DO NOT delete this file!
# It is necessary for linking the library.

# Name of the PIC object.
pic_object='.libs/foo.o'

# Name of the non-PIC object.
```

```
non_pic_object='foo.o'
```

Notice that the second run of GCC has its output discarded. This is done so that compiler warnings aren't annoyingly duplicated. If you need to see both sets of warnings (you might have conditional code inside '#ifdef PIC' for example), you can turn off suppression with the -no-suppress option to libtool's compile mode:

```
burger$ libtool --mode=compile gcc -no-suppress -g -O -c hello.c
gcc -g -O -c hello.c  -fPIC -DPIC -o .libs/hello.o
gcc -g -O -c hello.c -o hello.o
burger$
```

3.2 Linking libraries

Without libtool, the programmer would invoke the **ar** command to create a static library:

```
burger$ ar cru libhello.a hello.o foo.o
burger$
```

But of course, that would be too simple, so many systems require that you run the **ranlib** command on the resulting library (to give it better karma, or something):

```
burger$ ranlib libhello.a
burger$
```

It seems more natural to use the C compiler for this task, given libtool's "libraries are programs" approach. So, on platforms without shared libraries, libtool simply acts as a wrapper for the system **ar** (and possibly **ranlib**) commands.

Again, the libtool control file name (.la suffix) differs from the standard library name (.a suffix). The arguments to libtool are the same ones you would use to produce an executable named libhello.la with your compiler (see Section 4.2 [Link mode], page 18):

```
a23$ libtool --mode=link gcc -g -O -o libhello.la foo.o hello.o
*** Warning: Linking the shared library libhello.la against the
*** non-libtool objects foo.o hello.o is not portable!
ar cru .libs/libhello.a
ranlib .libs/libhello.a
creating libhello.la
(cd .libs && rm -f libhello.la && ln -s ../libhello.la libhello.la)
a23$
```

Aha! Libtool caught a common error... trying to build a library from standard objects instead of special .lo object files. This doesn't matter so much for static libraries, but on shared library systems, it is of great importance. (Note that you may replace libhello.la with libhello.a in which case libtool won't issue the warning any more. But although this method works, this is not intended to be used because it makes you lose the benefits of using Libtool.)

So, let's try again, this time with the library object files. Remember also that we need to add -lm to the link command line because **foo.c** uses the **cos** math library function (see Chapter 3 [Using libtool], page 4).

Another complication in building shared libraries is that we need to specify the path to the directory wher they will (eventually) be installed (in this case, `/usr/local/lib`)[1]:

```
a23$ libtool --mode=link gcc -g -O -o libhello.la foo.lo hello.lo \
             -rpath /usr/local/lib -lm
ar cru .libs/libhello.a foo.o hello.o
ranlib .libs/libhello.a
creating libhello.la
(cd .libs && rm -f libhello.la && ln -s ../libhello.la libhello.la)
a23$
```

Now, let's try the same trick on the shared library platform:

```
burger$ libtool --mode=link gcc -g -O -o libhello.la foo.lo hello.lo \
               -rpath /usr/local/lib -lm
rm -fr  .libs/libhello.a .libs/libhello.la
ld -Bshareable -o .libs/libhello.so.0.0 .libs/foo.o .libs/hello.o -lm
ar cru .libs/libhello.a foo.o hello.o
ranlib .libs/libhello.a
creating libhello.la
(cd .libs && rm -f libhello.la && ln -s ../libhello.la libhello.la)
burger$
```

Now that's significantly cooler... Libtool just ran an obscure `ld` command to create a shared library, as well as the static library.

Note how libtool creates extra files in the `.libs` subdirectory, rather than the current directory. This feature is to make it easier to clean up the build directory, and to help ensure that other programs fail horribly if you accidentally forget to use libtool when you should.

Again, you may want to have a look at the `.la` file to see what Libtool stores in it. In particular, you will see that Libtool uses this file to remember the destination directory for the library (the argument to **-rpath**) as well as the dependency on the math library ('**-lm**').

3.3 Linking executables

If you choose at this point to *install* the library (put it in a permanent location) before linking executables against it, then you don't need to use libtool to do the linking. Simply use the appropriate **-L** and **-l** flags to specify the library's location.

Some system linkers insist on encoding the full directory name of each shared library in the resulting executable. Libtool has to work around this misfeature by special magic to ensure that only permanent directory names are put into installed executables.

The importance of this bug must not be overlooked: it won't cause programs to crash in obvious ways. It creates a security hole, and possibly even worse, if you are modifying the library source code after you have installed the package, you will change the behaviour of the installed programs!

So, if you want to link programs against the library before you install it, you must use libtool to do the linking.

---

[1] If you don't specify an **rpath**, then libtool builds a libtool convenience archive, not a shared library (see Section 3.7 [Static libraries], page 13).

Here's the old way of linking against an uninstalled library:

```
burger$ gcc -g -O -o hell.old main.o libhello.a -lm
burger$
```

Libtool's way is almost the same[2] (see Section 4.2 [Link mode], page 18):

```
a23$ libtool --mode=link gcc -g -O -o hell main.o libhello.la
gcc -g -O -o hell main.o  ./.libs/libhello.a -lm
a23$
```

That looks too simple to be true. All libtool did was transform `libhello.la` to `./.libs/libhello.a`, but remember that 'a23' has no shared libraries. Notice that Libtool also remembered that `libhello.la` depends on `-lm`, so even though we didn't specify `-lm` on the libtool command line[3] Libtool has added it to the `gcc` link line for us.

On 'burger' Libtool links against the uninstalled shared library:

```
burger$ libtool --mode=link gcc -g -O -o hell main.o libhello.la
gcc -g -O -o .libs/hell main.o -L./.libs -R/usr/local/lib -lhello -lm
creating hell
burger$
```

Now assume `libhello.la` had already been installed, and you want to link a new program with it. You could figure out where it lives by yourself, then run:

```
burger$ gcc -g -O -o test test.o -L/usr/local/lib -lhello -lm
```

However, unless `/usr/local/lib` is in the standard library search path, you won't be able to run `test`. However, if you use libtool to link the already-installed libtool library, it will do The Right Thing (TM) for you:

```
burger$ libtool --mode=link gcc -g -O -o test test.o \
                /usr/local/lib/libhello.la
gcc -g -O -o .libs/test test.o -Wl,--rpath \
        -Wl,/usr/local/lib /usr/local/lib/libhello.a -lm
creating test
burger$
```

Note that libtool added the necessary run-time path flag, as well as `-lm`, the library libhello.la depended upon. Nice, huh?

Notice that the executable, `hell`, was actually created in the `.libs` subdirectory. Then, a wrapper script (or, on certain platforms, a wrapper executable see Section 3.3.1 [Wrapper executables], page 9) was created in the current directory.

Since libtool created a wrapper script, you should use libtool to install it and debug it too. However, since the program does not depend on any uninstalled libtool library, it is probably usable even without the wrapper script.

On NetBSD 1.2, libtool encodes the installation directory of `libhello`, by using the '-R/usr/local/lib' compiler flag. Then, the wrapper script guarantees that the executable finds the correct shared library (the one in `./.libs`) until it is properly installed.

Let's compare the two different programs:

---

[2] However, you should avoid using `-L` or `-l` flags to link against an uninstalled libtool library. Just specify the relative path to the `.la` file, such as `../intl/libintl.la`. This is a design decision to eliminate any ambiguity when linking against uninstalled shared libraries.

[3] And why should we? `main.o` doesn't directly depend on `-lm` after all.

```
burger$ time ./hell.old
Welcome to GNU Hell!
** This is not GNU Hello.  There is no built-in mail reader. **
        0.21 real         0.02 user         0.08 sys
burger$ time ./hell
Welcome to GNU Hell!
** This is not GNU Hello.  There is no built-in mail reader. **
        0.63 real         0.09 user         0.59 sys
burger$
```

The wrapper script takes significantly longer to execute, but at least the results are correct, even though the shared library hasn't been installed yet.

So, what about all the space savings that shared libraries are supposed to yield?

```
burger$ ls -l hell.old libhello.a
-rwxr-xr-x  1 gord  gord  15481 Nov 14 12:11 hell.old
-rw-r--r--  1 gord  gord   4274 Nov 13 18:02 libhello.a
burger$ ls -l .libs/hell .libs/libhello.*
-rwxr-xr-x  1 gord  gord  11647 Nov 14 12:10 .libs/hell
-rw-r--r--  1 gord  gord   4274 Nov 13 18:44 .libs/libhello.a
-rwxr-xr-x  1 gord  gord  12205 Nov 13 18:44 .libs/libhello.so.0.0
burger$
```

Well, that sucks. Maybe I should just scrap this project and take up basket weaving.

Actually, it just proves an important point: shared libraries incur overhead because of their (relative) complexity. In this situation, the price of being dynamic is eight kilobytes, and the payoff is about four kilobytes. So, having a shared libhello won't be an advantage until we link it against at least a few more programs.

3.3.1 Wrapper executables for uninstalled programs

Some platforms, notably those hosted on Windows such as Cygwin and MinGW, use a wrapper executable rather than a wrapper script to ensure proper operation of uninstalled programs linked by libtool against uninstalled shared libraries. The wrapper executable thus performs the same function as the wrapper script used on other platforms, but allows to satisfy the make rules for the program, whose name ends in $(EXEEXT). The actual program executable is created below .libs, and its name will end in $(EXEEXT) and may or may not contain an lt- prefix. This wrapper executable sets various environment values so that the program executable may locate its (uninstalled) shared libraries, and then launches the program executable.

The wrapper executable provides a debug mode, enabled by passing the command-line option --lt-debug (see below). When executing in debug mode, diagnostic information will be printed to stderr before the program executable is launched.

Finally, the wrapper executable supports a number of command line options that may be useful when debugging the operation of the wrapper system. All of these options begin with --lt-, and if present they and their arguments will be removed from the argument list passed on to the program executable. Therefore, the program executable may not employ command line options that begin with --lt-. (In fact, the wrapper executable will detect any command line options that begin with --lt- and abort with an error message if the option is not recognized). If this presents a problem, please contact the Libtool team at the Libtool bug reporting address `bug-libtool@gnu.org`.

These command line options include:

`--lt-dump-script`

> Causes the wrapper to print a copy of the wrapper *script* to `stdout`, and exit.

`--lt-debug`

> Causes the wrapper to print diagnostic information to `stdout`, before launching the program executable.

For consistency, both the wrapper *script* and the wrapper *executable* support these options.

3.4 Debugging executables

If `hell` was a complicated program, you would certainly want to test and debug it before installing it on your system. In the above section, you saw how the libtool wrapper script makes it possible to run the program directly, but unfortunately, this mechanism interferes with the debugger:

```
burger$ gdb hell
GDB is free software and you are welcome to distribute copies of it
 under certain conditions; type "show copying" to see the conditions.
There is no warranty for GDB; type "show warranty" for details.
GDB 4.16 (i386-unknown-netbsd), (C) 1996 Free Software Foundation, Inc.

"hell": not in executable format: File format not recognized

(gdb) quit
burger$
```

Sad. It doesn't work because GDB doesn't know where the executable lives. So, let's try again, by invoking GDB directly on the executable:

```
burger$ gdb .libs/hell
GNU gdb 5.3 (i386-unknown-netbsd)
Copyright 2002 Free Software Foundation, Inc.
GDB is free software, covered by the GNU General Public License,
and you are welcome to change it and/or distribute copies of it
under certain conditions.  Type "show copying" to see the conditions.
There is no warranty for GDB.  Type "show warranty" for details.
(gdb) break main
Breakpoint 1 at 0x8048547: file main.c, line 29.
(gdb) run
Starting program: /home/src/libtool/demo/.libs/hell
/home/src/libtool/demo/.libs/hell: can't load library 'libhello.so.0'

Program exited with code 020.
(gdb) quit
burger$
```

Argh. Now GDB complains because it cannot find the shared library that `hell` is linked against. So, we must use libtool to properly set the library path and run the debugger. Fortunately, we can forget all about the `.libs` directory, and just run it on the executable wrapper (see Section 4.3 [Execute mode], page 21):

```
burger$ libtool --mode=execute gdb hell
GNU gdb 5.3 (i386-unknown-netbsd)
Copyright 2002 Free Software Foundation, Inc.
GDB is free software, covered by the GNU General Public License,
and you are welcome to change it and/or distribute copies of it
under certain conditions.  Type "show copying" to see the conditions.
There is no warranty for GDB.  Type "show warranty" for details.
(gdb) break main
Breakpoint 1 at 0x8048547: file main.c, line 29.
(gdb) run
Starting program: /home/src/libtool/demo/.libs/hell

Breakpoint 1, main (argc=1, argv=0xbffffc40) at main.c:29
29          printf ("Welcome to GNU Hell!\n");
(gdb) quit
The program is running.  Quit anyway (and kill it)? (y or n) y
burger$
```

3.5 Installing libraries

Installing libraries on a non-libtool system is quite straightforward... just copy them into place:[4]

```
burger$ su
Password: ********
burger# cp libhello.a /usr/local/lib/libhello.a
burger#
```

Oops, don't forget the `ranlib` command:

```
burger# ranlib /usr/local/lib/libhello.a
burger#
```

Libtool installation is quite simple, as well. Just use the `install` or `cp` command that you normally would (see Section 4.4 [Install mode], page 22):

```
a23# libtool --mode=install cp libhello.la /usr/local/lib/libhello.la
cp libhello.la /usr/local/lib/libhello.la
cp .libs/libhello.a /usr/local/lib/libhello.a
ranlib /usr/local/lib/libhello.a
a23#
```

Note that the libtool library `libhello.la` is also installed, to help libtool with uninstallation (see Section 4.6 [Uninstall mode], page 23) and linking (see Section 3.3 [Linking executables], page 7) and to help programs with dlopening (see Chapter 10 [Dlopened modules], page 48).

---

[4] Don't strip static libraries though, or they will be unusable.

Here is the shared library example:

```
burger# libtool --mode=install install -c libhello.la \
                /usr/local/lib/libhello.la
install -c .libs/libhello.so.0.0 /usr/local/lib/libhello.so.0.0
install -c libhello.la /usr/local/lib/libhello.la
install -c .libs/libhello.a /usr/local/lib/libhello.a
ranlib /usr/local/lib/libhello.a
burger#
```

It is safe to specify the -s (strip symbols) flag if you use a BSD-compatible install program when installing libraries. Libtool will either ignore the -s flag, or will run a program that will strip only debugging and compiler symbols from the library.

Once the libraries have been put in place, there may be some additional configuration that you need to do before using them. First, you must make sure that where the library is installed actually agrees with the -rpath flag you used to build it.

Then, running 'libtool -n finish *libdir*' can give you further hints on what to do (see Section 4.5 [Finish mode], page 22):

```
burger# libtool -n finish /usr/local/lib
PATH="$PATH:/sbin" ldconfig -m /usr/local/lib
----------------------------------------------------------------

Libraries have been installed in:
   /usr/local/lib


To link against installed libraries in a given directory, LIBDIR,
you must use the '-LLIBDIR' flag during linking.

  You will also need to do one of the following:
    - add LIBDIR to the 'LD_LIBRARY_PATH' environment variable
      during execution
    - add LIBDIR to the 'LD_RUN_PATH' environment variable
      during linking
    - use the '-RLIBDIR' linker flag


See any operating system documentation about shared libraries for
more information, such as the ld and ld.so manual pages.
----------------------------------------------------------------
burger#
```

After you have completed these steps, you can go on to begin using the installed libraries. You may also install any executables that depend on libraries you created.

3.6 Installing executables

If you used libtool to link any executables against uninstalled libtool libraries (see Section 3.3 [Linking executables], page 7), you need to use libtool to install the executables after the libraries have been installed (see Section 3.5 [Installing libraries], page 11).

So, for our Ultrix example, we would run:

```
a23# libtool --mode=install -c hell /usr/local/bin/hell
install -c hell /usr/local/bin/hell
a23#
```

On shared library systems that require wrapper scripts, libtool just ignores the wrapper script and installs the correct binary:

```
burger# libtool --mode=install -c hell /usr/local/bin/hell
install -c .libs/hell /usr/local/bin/hell
burger#
```

3.7 Linking static libraries

Why return to **ar** and **ranlib** silliness when you've had a taste of libtool? Well, sometimes it is desirable to create a static archive that can never be shared. The most frequent case is when you have a set of object files that you use to build several different libraries. You can create a "convenience library" out of those objects, and link against that with the other libraries, instead of listing all the object files every time.

If you just want to link this convenience library into programs, then you could just ignore libtool entirely, and use the old **ar** and **ranlib** commands (or the corresponding GNU Automake '**_LIBRARIES**' rules). You can even install a convenience library using GNU Libtool, though you probably don't want to and hence GNU Automake doesn't allow you to do so.

```
burger$ libtool --mode=install ./install-sh -c libhello.a \
               /local/lib/libhello.a
./install-sh -c libhello.a /local/lib/libhello.a
ranlib /local/lib/libhello.a
burger$
```

Using libtool for static library installation protects your library from being accidentally stripped (if the installer used the **-s** flag), as well as automatically running the correct **ranlib** command.

But libtool libraries are more than just collections of object files: they can also carry library dependency information, which old archives do not. If you want to create a libtool static convenience library, you can omit the **-rpath** flag and use **-static** to indicate that you're only interested in a static library. When you link a program with such a library, libtool will actually link all object files and dependency libraries into the program.

If you omit both **-rpath** and **-static**, libtool will create a convenience library that can be used to create other libtool libraries, even shared ones. Just like in the static case, the library behaves as an alias to a set of object files and dependency libraries, but in this case the object files are suitable for inclusion in shared libraries. But be careful not to link a single convenience library, directly or indirectly, into a single program or library, otherwise you may get errors about symbol redefinitions.

The key is remembering that a convenience library contains PIC objects, and can be linked where a list of PIC objects makes sense; i.e. into a shared library. A static convenience library contains non-PIC objects, so can be linked into an old static library, or a program.

When GNU Automake is used, you should use **noinst_LTLIBRARIES** instead of **lib_LTLIBRARIES** for convenience libraries, so that the **-rpath** option is not passed when they are linked.

As a rule of thumb, link a libtool convenience library into at most one libtool library, and never into a program, and link libtool static convenience libraries only into programs, and only if you need to carry library dependency information to the user of the static convenience library.

Another common situation where static linking is desirable is in creating a standalone binary. Use libtool to do the linking and add the **-all-static** flag.

4 Invoking `libtool`

The `libtool` program has the following synopsis:

    libtool [option]... [mode-arg]...

and accepts the following options:

`--config`   Display libtool configuration variables and exit.

`--debug`   Dump a trace of shell script execution to standard output. This produces a lot of output, so you may wish to pipe it to `less` (or `more`) or redirect to a file.

`-n`
`--dry-run`
> Don't create, modify, or delete any files, just show what commands would be executed by libtool.

`--features`
> Display basic configuration options. This provides a way for packages to determine whether shared or static libraries will be built.

`--finish`   Same as `--mode=finish`.

`-h`   Display short help message.

`--help`   Display a help message and exit. If `--mode=mode` is specified, then detailed help for *mode* is displayed.

`--help-all`
> Display help for the general options as well as detailed help for each operation mode, and exit.

`--mode=mode`
> Use *mode* as the operation mode. When using libtool from the command line, you can give just *mode* (or a unique abbreviation of it) as the first argument as a shorthand for the full `--mode=mode`. For example, the following are equivalent:
>
> $ libtool --mode=execute --dry-run gdb prog.exe
> $ libtool   execute --dry-run gdb prog.exe
> $ libtool   exe   --dry-run gdb prog.exe
> $ libtool   e   --dry-run gdb prog.exe
>
> *mode* must be set to one of the following:

compile   Compile a source file into a libtool object.

execute   Automatically set the library path so that another program can use uninstalled libtool-generated programs or libraries.

link   Create a library or an executable.

install   Install libraries or executables.

finish   Complete the installation of libtool libraries on the system.

uninstall
> Delete installed libraries or executables.

clean   Delete uninstalled libraries or executables.

`--tag=tag`

Use configuration variables from tag *tag* (see Section 6.2 [Tags], page 39).

`--preserve-dup-deps`

Do not remove duplicate dependencies in libraries. When building packages with static libraries, the libraries may depend circularly on each other (shared libs can too, but for those it doesn't matter), so there are situations, where -la -lb -la is required, and the second -la may not be stripped or the link will fail. In cases where these duplications are required, this option will preserve them, only stripping the libraries that libtool knows it can safely.

`--quiet`
`--silent`   Do not print out any progress or informational messages.

`-v`
`--verbose`

Print out progress and informational messages (enabled by default), as well as additional messages not ordinary seen by default.

`--no-quiet`
`--no-silent`

Print out the progress and informational messages that are seen by default. This option has no effect on whether the additional messages seen in `--verbose` mode are shown.

`--no-verbose`

Do not print out any additional informational messages beyond those ordinarily seen by default. This option has no effect on whether the ordinary progress and informational messages enabled by `--no-quiet` are shown.

Thus, there are now three different message levels (not counting `--debug`), depending on whether the normal messages and/or the additional verbose messages are displayed. Note that there is no mechanism to display verbose messages, without also displaying normal messages.

default   Normal messages are displayed, verbose messages are not displayed. In addition to being the default mode, it can be forcibly achieved by using both option `--no-verbose` and either option `--no-silent` or option `--no-quiet`.

silent   Neither normal messages nor verbose messages are displayed. This mode can be achieved using either option `--silent` or option `--quiet`.

verbose   Both normal messages and verbose messages are displayed. This mode can be achieved using either option `-v` or option `--verbose`.

`--version`
Print libtool version information and exit.

The current `libtool` implementation is done with a shell script that needs to be invoked by the shell that `configure` chose for configuring `libtool` (see Section "The Autoconf

Manual" in *The Autoconf Manual*). This shell is set in the she-bang ('#!') line of the libtool script. Using a different shell may cause undefined behavior.

The *mode-args* are a variable number of arguments, depending on the selected operation mode. In general, each *mode-arg* is interpreted by programs libtool invokes, rather than libtool itself.

4.1 Compile mode

For *compile* mode, *mode-args* is a compiler command to be used in creating a "standard" object file. These arguments should begin with the name of the C compiler, and contain the -c compiler flag so that only an object file is created.

Libtool determines the name of the output file by removing the directory component from the source file name, then substituting the source code suffix (e.g. '.c' for C source code) with the library object suffix, '.lo'.

If shared libraries are being built, any necessary PIC generation flags are substituted into the compilation command.

The following components of *mode-args* are treated specially:

-o
    Note that the -o option is now fully supported. It is emulated on the platforms that don't support it (by locking and moving the objects), so it is really easy to use libtool, just with minor modifications to your Makefiles. Typing for example

        `libtool --mode=compile gcc -c foo/x.c -o foo/x.lo`

    will do what you expect.

    Note, however, that, if the compiler does not support -c and -o, it is impossible to compile foo/x.c without overwriting an existing ./x.o. Therefore, if you do have a source file ./x.c, make sure you introduce dependencies in your Makefile to make sure ./x.o (or ./x.lo) is re-created after any sub-directory's x.lo:

        `x.o x.lo: foo/x.lo bar/x.lo`

    This will also ensure that make won't try to use a temporarily corrupted x.o to create a program or library. It may cause needless recompilation on platforms that support -c and -o together, but it's the only way to make it safe for those that don't.

-no-suppress
    If both PIC and non-PIC objects are being built, libtool will normally suppress the compiler output for the PIC object compilation to save showing very similar, if not identical duplicate output for each object. If the -no-suppress option is given in compile mode, libtool will show the compiler output for both objects.

-prefer-pic
    Libtool will try to build only PIC objects.

-prefer-non-pic
    Libtool will try to build only non-PIC objects.

-shared   Even if Libtool was configured with --enable-static, the object file Libtool
           builds will not be suitable for static linking. Libtool will signal an error if it
           was configured with --disable-shared, or if the host does not support shared
           libraries.

-static   Even if libtool was configured with --disable-static, the object file Libtool
           builds **will** be suitable for static linking.

-Wc,*flag*
-Xcompiler *flag*

           Pass a flag directly to the compiler. With -Wc,, multiple flags may be separated
           by commas, whereas -Xcompiler passes through commas unchanged.

4.2 Link mode

Link mode links together object files (including library objects) to form another library or
to create an executable program.

   mode-args consist of a command using the C compiler to create an output file (with the
-o flag) from several object files.

   The following components of *mode-args* are treated specially:

-all-static
           If *output-file* is a program, then do not link it against any shared libraries at all.
           If *output-file* is a library, then only create a static library. In general, this flag
           cannot be used together with 'disable-static' (see Section 5.4.1 [LT_INIT],
           page 27).

-avoid-version
           Tries to avoid versioning (see Chapter 7 [Versioning], page 41) for libraries and
           modules, i.e. no version information is stored and no symbolic links are created.
           If the platform requires versioning, this option has no effect.

-bindir   Pass the absolute name of the directory for installing executable programs (see
           Section "Directory Variables" in *The GNU Coding Standards*). libtool may
           use this value to install shared libraries there on systems that do not provide
           for any library hardcoding and use the directory of a program and the PATH
           variable as library search path. This is typically used for DLLs on Windows or
           other systems using the PE (Portable Executable) format. On other systems,
           -bindir is ignored. The default value used is *libdir*/../bin for libraries
           installed to *libdir*. You should not use -bindir for modules.

-dlopen *file*
           Same as -dlpreopen *file*, if native dlopening is not supported on the host
           platform (see Chapter 10 [Dlopened modules], page 48) or if the program is
           linked with -static, -static-libtool-libs, or -all-static. Otherwise, no
           effect. If *file* is self Libtool will make sure that the program can dlopen itself,
           either by enabling -export-dynamic or by falling back to -dlpreopen self.

-dlpreopen *file*
           Link *file* into the output program, and add its symbols to the list of preloaded
           symbols (see Section 10.2 [Dlpreopening], page 49). If *file* is self, the symbols

of the program itself will be added to preloaded symbol lists. If *file* is `force` Libtool will make sure that a preloaded symbol list is always *defined*, regardless of whether it's empty or not.

`-export-dynamic`

Allow symbols from *output-file* to be resolved with `dlsym` (see Chapter 10 [Dlopened modules], page 48).

`-export-symbols` *symfile*

Tells the linker to export only the symbols listed in *symfile*. The symbol file should end in `.sym` and must contain the name of one symbol per line. This option has no effect on some platforms. By default all symbols are exported.

`-export-symbols-regex` *regex*

Same as `-export-symbols`, except that only symbols matching the regular expression *regex* are exported. By default all symbols are exported.

`-L`*libdir*   Search *libdir* for required libraries that have already been installed.

`-l`*name*   *output-file* requires the installed library `lib`*name*. This option is required even when *output-file* is not an executable.

`-module`   Creates a library that can be dlopened (see Chapter 10 [Dlopened modules], page 48). This option doesn't work for programs. Module names don't need to be prefixed with 'lib'. In order to prevent name clashes, however, `lib`*name* and **name** must not be used at the same time in your package.

`-no-fast-install`

Disable fast-install mode for the executable *output-file*. Useful if the program won't be necessarily installed.

`-no-install`

Link an executable *output-file* that can't be installed and therefore doesn't need a wrapper script on systems that allow hardcoding of library paths. Useful if the program is only used in the build tree, e.g., for testing or generating other files.

`-no-undefined`

Declare that *output-file* does not depend on any libraries other than the ones listed on the command line, i.e., after linking, it will not have unresolved symbols. Some platforms require all symbols in shared libraries to be resolved at library creation (see Chapter 9 [Inter-library dependencies], page 47), and using this parameter allows `libtool` to assume that this will not happen.

`-o` *output-file*

Create *output-file* from the specified objects and libraries.

`-objectlist` *file*

Use a list of object files found in *file* to specify objects.

`-os2dllname` *name*

Use this to change the DLL base name on OS/2 to *name*, to keep within the 8 character base name limit on this system.

`-precious-files-regex regex`

> Prevents removal of files from the temporary output directory whose names match this regular expression. You might specify '\.bbg?$' to keep those files created with gcc -ftest-coverage for example.

`-release release`

> Specify that the library was generated by release *release* of your package, so that users can easily tell what versions are newer than others. Be warned that no two releases of your package will be binary compatible if you use this flag. If you want binary compatibility, use the **-version-info** flag instead (see Chapter 7 [Versioning], page 41).

`-rpath libdir`

> If *output-file* is a library, it will eventually be installed in *libdir*. If *output-file* is a program, add *libdir* to the run-time path of the program. On platforms that don't support hardcoding library paths into executables and only search PATH for shared libraries, such as when *output-file* is a Windows (or other PE platform) DLL, the `.la` control file will be installed in *libdir*, but see **-bindir** above for the eventual destination of the `.dll` or other library file itself.

`-R libdir` If *output-file* is a program, add *libdir* to its run-time path. If *output-file* is a library, add **-R***libdir* to its *dependency_libs*, so that, whenever the library is linked into a program, *libdir* will be added to its run-time path.

`-shared` If *output-file* is a program, then link it against any uninstalled shared libtool libraries (this is the default behavior). If *output-file* is a library, then only create a shared library. In the later case, libtool will signal an error if it was configured with **--disable-shared**, or if the host does not support shared libraries.

`-shrext suffix`

> If *output-file* is a libtool library, replace the system's standard file name extension for shared libraries with *suffix* (most systems use `.so` here). This option is helpful in certain cases where an application requires that shared libraries (typically modules) have an extension other than the default one. Please note you must supply the full file name extension including any leading dot.

`-static` If *output-file* is a program, then do not link it against any uninstalled shared libtool libraries. If *output-file* is a library, then only create a static library.

`-static-libtool-libs`

> If *output-file* is a program, then do not link it against any shared libtool libraries. If *output-file* is a library, then only create a static library.

`-version-info current[:revision[:age]]`

> If *output-file* is a libtool library, use interface version information *current*, *revision*, and *age* to build it (see Chapter 7 [Versioning], page 41). Do **not** use this flag to specify package release information, rather see the **-release** flag.

`-version-number major[:minor[:revision]]`

> If *output-file* is a libtool library, compute interface version information so that the resulting library uses the specified major, minor and revision numbers. This

is designed to permit libtool to be used with existing projects where identical version numbers are already used across operating systems. New projects should use the `-version-info` flag instead.

`-weak` *libname*

if *output-file* is a libtool library, declare that it provides a weak *libname* interface. This is a hint to libtool that there is no need to append *libname* to the list of dependency libraries of *output-file*, because linking against *output-file* already supplies the same interface (see Section 10.3 [Linking with dlopened modules], page 51).

`-Wc,`*flag*
`-Xcompiler` *flag*

Pass a linker-specific flag directly to the compiler. With `-Wc,`, multiple flags may be separated by commas, whereas `-Xcompiler` passes through commas unchanged.

`-Wl,`*flag*
`-Xlinker` *flag*

Pass a linker-specific flag directly to the linker.

`-XCClinker` *flag*

Pass a link-specific flag to the compiler driver (`CC`) during linking.

If the *output-file* ends in `.la`, then a libtool library is created, which must be built only from library objects (`.lo` files). The `-rpath` option is required. In the current implementation, libtool libraries may not depend on other uninstalled libtool libraries (see Chapter 9 [Inter-library dependencies], page 47).

If the *output-file* ends in `.a`, then a standard library is created using `ar` and possibly `ranlib`.

If *output-file* ends in `.o` or `.lo`, then a reloadable object file is created from the input files (generally using '`ld -r`'). This method is often called *partial linking*.

Otherwise, an executable program is created.

4.3 Execute mode

For *execute* mode, the library path is automatically set, then a program is executed.

The first of the *mode-args* is treated as a program name, with the rest as arguments to that program.

The following components of *mode-args* are treated specially:

`-dlopen` *file*

Add the directory containing *file* to the library path.

This mode sets the library path environment variable according to any `-dlopen` flags.

If any of the *args* are libtool executable wrappers, then they are translated into the name of their corresponding uninstalled binary, and any of their required library directories are added to the library path.

4.4 Install mode

In *install* mode, libtool interprets most of the elements of *mode-args* as an installation command beginning with `cp`, or a BSD-compatible `install` program.

The following components of *mode-args* are treated specially:

`-inst-prefix-dir` *inst-prefix-dir*

When installing into a temporary staging area, rather than the final `prefix`, this argument is used to reflect the temporary path, in much the same way `automake` uses DESTDIR. For instance, if `prefix` is `/usr/local`, but *inst-prefix-dir* is `/tmp`, then the object will be installed under `/tmp/usr/local/`. If the installed object is a libtool library, then the internal fields of that library will reflect only `prefix`, not *inst-prefix-dir*:

```
# Directory that this library needs to be installed in:
libdir='/usr/local/lib'
```

not

```
# Directory that this library needs to be installed in:
libdir='/tmp/usr/local/lib'
```

inst-prefix is also used to ensure that if the installed object must be re-linked upon installation, that it is relinked against the libraries in *inst prefix dir*/`prefix`, not `prefix`.

In truth, this option is not really intended for use when calling libtool directly; it is automatically used when `libtool --mode=install` calls `libtool --mode=relink`. Libtool does this by analyzing the destination path given in the original `libtool --mode=install` command and comparing it to the expected installation path established during `libtool --mode=link`.

Thus, end-users need change nothing, and `automake`-style `make install DESTDIR=/tmp` will Just Work(tm) most of the time. For systems where fast installation cannot be turned on, relinking may be needed. In this case, a 'DESTDIR' install will fail.

Currently it is not generally possible to install into a temporary staging area that contains needed third-party libraries that are not yet visible at their final location.

The rest of the *mode-args* are interpreted as arguments to the `cp` or `install` command.

The command is run, and any necessary unprivileged post-installation commands are also completed.

4.5 Finish mode

Finish mode has two functions. One is to help system administrators install libtool libraries so that they can be located and linked into user programs. To invoke this functionality, pass the name of a library directory as *mode-arg*. Running this command may require superuser privileges, and the `--dry-run` option may be useful.

The second is to facilitate transferring libtool libraries to a native compilation environment after they were built in a cross-compilation environment. Cross-compilation environments may rely on recent libtool features, and running libtool in finish mode will make it easier to work with older versions of libtool. This task is performed whenever the *mode-arg* is a `.la` file.

4.6 Uninstall mode

Uninstall mode deletes installed libraries, executables and objects.

The first *mode-arg* is the name of the program to use to delete files (typically `/bin/rm`).

The remaining *mode-args* are either flags for the deletion program (beginning with a '-'), or the names of files to delete.

4.7 Clean mode

Clean mode deletes uninstalled libraries, executables, objects and libtool's temporary files associated with them.

The first *mode-arg* is the name of the program to use to delete files (typically `/bin/rm`).

The remaining *mode-args* are either flags for the deletion program (beginning with a '-'), or the names of files to delete.

5 Integrating libtool with your package

This chapter describes how to integrate libtool with your packages so that your users can install hassle-free shared libraries.

There are several ways that Libtool may be integrated in your package, described in the following sections. Typically, the Libtool macro files as well as `ltmain.sh` are copied into your package using `libtoolize` and `aclocal` after setting up the `configure.ac` and toplevel `Makefile.am`, then `autoconf` adds the needed tests to the `configure` script. These individual steps are often automated with `autoreconf`.

Here is a diagram showing how such a typical Libtool configuration works when preparing a package for distribution, assuming that `m4` has been chosen as location for additional Autoconf macros, and `build-aux` as location for auxiliary build tools (see Section "The Autoconf Manual" in *The Autoconf Manual*):

```
libtool.m4 -----.                    .--> aclocal.m4 -----.
ltoptions.m4 ---+  .-> aclocal* -+                        +--> autoconf*
ltversion.m4 ---+--+             '--> [copy in m4/] --+        |
ltsugar.m4     ¦  |                        ^          |        \/
lt~obsolete.m4 -+  +-> libtoolize* -----'             |     configure
[ltdl.m4] ------+  |                                  |
                   '---------------------------------'

ltmain.sh -----------> libtoolize* -> [copy in build-aux/]
```

During configuration, the `libtool` script is generated either through `config.status` or `config.lt`:

```
              .--> config.status* --.
configure* --+                       +--> libtool
              '--> [config.lt*] ----'         ^
                                              |
ltmain.sh -----------------------------------'
```

At `make` run time, `libtool` is then invoked as needed as a wrapper around compilers, linkers, install and cleanup programs.

There are alternatives choices to several parts of the setup; for example, the Libtool macro files can either be copied or symlinked into the package, or copied into `aclocal.m4`. As another example, an external, pre-configured `libtool` script may be used, by-passing most of the tests and package-specific setup for Libtool.

5.1 Autoconf macros exported by libtool

Libtool uses a number of macros to interrogate the host system when it is being built, and you can use some of them yourself too. Although there are a great many other macros in the libtool installed m4 files, these do not form part of the published interface, and are subject to change between releases.

Macros in the 'LT_CMD_' namespace check for various shell commands:

LT_CMD_MAX_LEN   [Macro]
> Finds the longest command line that can be safely passed to '$SHELL' without being
> truncated, and store in the shell variable '$max_cmd_len'. It is only an approximate
> value, but command lines of this length or shorter are guaranteed not to be truncated.

Macros in the 'LT_FUNC_' namespace check characteristics of library functions:

LT_FUNC_DLSYM_USCORE   [Macro]
> 'AC_DEFINE' the preprocessor symbol 'DLSYM_USCORE' if we have to add an underscore
> to symbol-names passed in to 'dlsym'.

Macros in the 'LT_LIB_' namespace check characteristics of system libraries:

LT_LIB_M   [Macro]
> Set 'LIBM' to the math library or libraries required on this machine, if any.

LT_LIB_DLLOAD   [Macro]
> This is the macro used by 'libltdl' to determine what dlloaders to use on this ma-
> chine, if any. Several shell variables are set (and 'AC_SUBST'ed) depending on the
> dlload interfaces are available on this machine. 'LT_DLLOADERS' contains a list of
> libtool libraries that can be used, and if necessary also sets 'LIBADD_DLOPEN' if addi-
> tional system libraries are required by the 'dlopen' loader, and 'LIBADD_SHL_LOAD'
> if additional system libraries are required by the 'shl_load' loader, respectively. Fi-
> nally some symbols are set in config.h depending on the loaders that are found to
> work: 'HAVE_LIBDL', 'HAVE_SHL_LOAD', 'HAVE_DYLD', 'HAVE_DLD'.

Macros in the 'LT_PATH_' namespace search the system for the full path to particular system
commands:

LT_PATH_LD   [Macro]
> Add a --with-gnu-ld option to configure. Try to find the path to the linker used
> by '$CC', and whether it is the GNU linker. The result is stored in the shell variable
> '$LD', which is AC_SUBSTed.

LT_PATH_NM   [Macro]
> Try to find a BSD-compatible nm or a MS-compatible dumpbin command on this
> machine. The result is stored in the shell variable '$NM', which is AC_SUBSTed.

Macros in the 'LT_SYS_' namespace probe for system characteristics:

LT_SYS_DLOPEN_SELF   [Macro]
> Tests whether a program can dlopen itself, and then also whether the same program
> can still dlopen itself when statically linked. Results are stored in the shell variables
> '$enable_dlopen_self' and 'enable_dlopen_self_static' respectively.

LT_SYS_DLOPEN_DEPLIBS   [Macro]
> Define the preprocessor symbol 'LTDL_DLOPEN_DEPLIBS' if the OS needs help to load
> dependent libraries for 'dlopen' (or equivalent).

LT_SYS_DLSEARCH_PATH   [Macro]
> Define the preprocessor symbol 'LT_DLSEARCH_PATH' to the system default library
> search path.

LT_SYS_MODULE_EXT   [Macro]
> Define the preprocessor symbol 'LT_MODULE_EXT' to the extension used for runtime loadable modules. If you use libltdl to open modules, then you can simply use the libtool library extension, .la.

LT_SYS_MODULE_PATH   [Macro]
> Define the preprocessor symbol 'LT_MODULE_PATH_VAR' to the name of the shell environment variable that determines the run-time module search path.

LT_SYS_SYMBOL_USCORE   [Macro]
> Set the shell variable 'sys_symbol_underscore' to 'no' unless the compiler prefixes global symbols with an underscore.

5.2 Writing `Makefile` rules for libtool

Libtool is fully integrated with Automake (see Section "Introduction" in *The Automake Manual*), starting with Automake version 1.2.

If you want to use libtool in a regular `Makefile` (or `Makefile.in`), you are on your own. If you're not using Automake, and you don't know how to incorporate libtool into your package you need to do one of the following:

1. Download the latest Automake distribution from your nearest GNU mirror, install it, and start using it.

2. Learn how to write `Makefile` rules by hand. They're sometimes complex, but if you're clever enough to write rules for compiling your old libraries, then you should be able to figure out new rules for libtool libraries (hint: examine the `Makefile.in` in the `tests/demo` subdirectory of the libtool distribution... note especially that it was automatically generated from the `Makefile.am` by Automake).

5.3 Using Automake with libtool

Libtool library support is implemented under the 'LTLIBRARIES' primary.

Here are some samples from the Automake `Makefile.am` in the libtool distribution's `demo` subdirectory.

First, to link a program against a libtool library, just use the 'program_LDADD'[1] variable:

```
bin_PROGRAMS = hell hell_static

# Build hell from main.c and libhello.la
hell_SOURCES = main.c
hell_LDADD = libhello.la
```

---

[1] Since GNU Automake 1.5, the flags -dlopen or -dlpreopen (see Section 4.2 [Link mode], page 18) can be employed with the 'program_LDADD' variable. Unfortunately, older releases didn't accept these flags, so if you are stuck with an ancient Automake, we recommend quoting the flag itself, and setting 'program_DEPENDENCIES' too:

```
program_LDADD = "-dlopen" libfoo.la
program_DEPENDENCIES = libfoo.la
```

```
# Create a statically linked version of hell.
hell_static_SOURCES = main.c
hell_static_LDADD = libhello.la
hell_static_LDFLAGS = -static
```

You may use the 'program_LDFLAGS' variable to stuff in any flags you want to pass to libtool while linking **program** (such as **-static** to avoid linking uninstalled shared libtool libraries).

Building a libtool library is almost as trivial... note the use of 'libhello_la_LDFLAGS' to pass the **-version-info** (see Chapter 7 [Versioning], page 41) option to libtool:

```
# Build a libtool library, libhello.la for installation in libdir.
lib_LTLIBRARIES = libhello.la
libhello_la_SOURCES = hello.c foo.c
libhello_la_LDFLAGS = -version-info 3:12:1
```

The **-rpath** option is passed automatically by Automake (except for libraries listed as **noinst_LTLIBRARIES**), so you should not specify it.

See Section "The Automake Manual" in *The Automake Manual*, for more information.

5.4 Configuring libtool

Libtool requires intimate knowledge of your compiler suite and operating system to be able to create shared libraries and link against them properly. When you install the libtool distribution, a system-specific libtool script is installed into your binary directory.

However, when you distribute libtool with your own packages (see Section 5.5 [Distributing], page 34), you do not always know the compiler suite and operating system that are used to compile your package.

For this reason, libtool must be *configured* before it can be used. This idea should be familiar to anybody who has used a GNU **configure** script. **configure** runs a number of tests for system features, then generates the **Makefiles** (and possibly a **config.h** header file), after which you can run **make** and build the package.

Libtool adds its own tests to your **configure** script to generate a libtool script for the installer's host machine.

5.4.1 The LT_INIT macro

If you are using GNU Autoconf (or Automake), you should add a call to **LT_INIT** to your **configure.ac** file. This macro adds many new tests to the **configure** script so that the generated libtool script will understand the characteristics of the host. It's the most important of a number of macros defined by Libtool:

LT_PREREQ (*version*)   [Macro]
  Ensure that a recent enough version of Libtool is being used. If the version of Libtool used for **LT_INIT** is earlier than *version*, print an error message to the standard error output and exit with failure (exit status is 63). For example:

```
LT_PREREQ([2.4.6])
```

LT_INIT (*options*)   [Macro]
AC_PROG_LIBTOOL   [Macro]

`AM_PROG_LIBTOOL`   [Macro]

Add support for the `--enable-shared`, `--disable-shared`, `--enable-static`, `--disable-static`, `--with-pic`, and `--without-pic` configure flags.[2] `AC_PROG_LIBTOOL` and `AM_PROG_LIBTOOL` are deprecated names for older versions of this macro; `autoupdate` will upgrade your `configure.ac` files.

By default, this macro turns on shared libraries if they are available, and also enables static libraries if they don't conflict with the shared libraries. You can modify these defaults by passing either `disable-shared` or `disable-static` in the option list to `LT_INIT`, or using `AC_DISABLE_SHARED` or `AC_DISABLE_STATIC`.

```
# Turn off shared libraries during beta-testing, since they
# make the build process take too long.
LT_INIT([disable-shared])
```

The user may specify modified forms of the configure flags `--enable-shared` and `--enable-static` to choose whether shared or static libraries are built based on the name of the package. For example, to have shared 'bfd' and 'gdb' libraries built, but not shared 'libg++', you can run all three `configure` scripts as follows:

```
trick$ ./configure --enable-shared=bfd,gdb
```

In general, specifying `--enable-shared=`*pkgs* is the same as configuring with `--enable-shared` every package named in the comma-separated *pkgs* list, and every other package with `--disable-shared`. The `--enable-static=`*pkgs* flag behaves similarly, but it uses `--enable-static` and `--disable-static`. The same applies to the `--enable-fast-install=`*pkgs* flag, which uses `--enable-fast-install` and `--disable-fast-install`.

The package name 'default' matches any packages that have not set their name in the `PACKAGE` environment variable.

The `--with-pic` and `--without-pic` configure flags can be used to specify whether or not `libtool` uses PIC objects. By default, `libtool` uses PIC objects for shared libraries and non-PIC objects for static libraries. The `--with-pic` option also accepts a comma-separated list of package names. Specifying `--with-pic=`*pkgs* is the same as configuring every package in *pkgs* with `--with-pic` and every other package with the default configuration. The package name 'default' is treated the same as for `--enable-shared` and `--enable-static`.

This macro also sets the shell variable `LIBTOOL_DEPS`, that you can use to automatically update the libtool script if it becomes out-of-date. In order to do that, add to your `configure.ac`:

```
LT_INIT
AC_SUBST([LIBTOOL_DEPS])
```

and, to `Makefile.in` or `Makefile.am`:

```
LIBTOOL_DEPS = @LIBTOOL_DEPS@
libtool: $(LIBTOOL_DEPS)
        $(SHELL) ./config.status libtool
```

---

[2] `LT_INIT` requires that you define the `Makefile` variable `top_builddir` in your `Makefile.in`. Automake does this automatically, but Autoconf users should set it to the relative path to the top of your build directory (`../..`, for example).

If you are using GNU Automake, you can omit the assignment, as Automake will take care of it. You'll obviously have to create some dependency on `libtool`.

Aside from `disable-static` and `disable-shared`, there are other options that you can pass to `LT_INIT` to modify its behaviour. Here is a full list:

'dlopen'　Enable checking for dlopen support. This option should be used if the package makes use of the `-dlopen` and `-dlpreopen` libtool flags, otherwise libtool will assume that the system does not support dlopening.

'win32-dll'

This option should be used if the package has been ported to build clean dlls on win32 platforms. Usually this means that any library data items are exported with `__declspec(dllexport)` and imported with `__declspec(dllimport)`. If this macro is not used, libtool will assume that the package libraries are not dll clean and will build only static libraries on win32 hosts.

Provision must be made to pass `-no-undefined` to `libtool` in link mode from the package `Makefile`. Naturally, if you pass `-no-undefined`, you must ensure that all the library symbols **really are** defined at link time!

'aix-soname=aix'
'aix-soname=svr4'
'aix-soname=both'

Enable the `--with-aix-soname` to `configure`, which the user can pass to override the given default.

By default (and **always** in releases prior to 2.4.4), Libtool always behaves as if `aix-soname=aix` is given, with no `configure` option for the user to override. Specifically, when the `-brtl` linker flag is seen in `LDFLAGS` at build-time, static archives are built from static objects only, otherwise, traditional AIX shared library archives of shared objects using in-archive versioning are built (with the `.a` file extension!). Similarly, with `-brtl` in `LDFLAGS`, libtool shared archives are built from shared objects, without any filename-based versioning; and without `-brtl` no shared archives are built at all.

When `aix-soname=svr4` option is given, or the `--with-aix-soname=svr4` `configure` option is passed, static archives are always created from static objects, even without `-brtl` in `LDFLAGS`. Shared archives are made from shared objects, and filename based versioning is enabled.

When `aix-soname=both` option is given, or the `--with-aix-soname=svr4` `configure` option is passed, static archives are built traditionally (as `aix-soname=aix`), and both kinds of shared archives are built. The `.la` pseudo-archive specifies one or the other depending on whether `-brtl` is specified in `LDFLAGS` when the library is built.

'disable-fast-install'

Change the default behaviour for `LT_INIT` to disable optimization for fast installation. The user may still override this default, depending on platform support, by specifying `--enable-fast-install` to `configure`.

'shared'   Change the default behaviour for LT_INIT to enable shared libraries.
              This is the default on all systems where Libtool knows how to create
              shared libraries. The user may still override this default by specifying
              --disable-shared to configure.

'disable-shared'
              Change the default behaviour for LT_INIT to disable shared libraries.
              The user may still override this default by specifying --enable-shared
              to configure.

'static'   Change the default behaviour for LT_INIT to enable static libraries. This
              is the default on all systems where shared libraries have been disabled
              for some reason, and on most systems where shared libraries have been
              enabled. If shared libraries are enabled, the user may still override this
              default by specifying --disable-static to configure.

'disable-static'
              Change the default behaviour for LT_INIT to disable static libraries. The
              user may still override this default by specifying --enable-static to
              configure.

'pic-only'
              Change the default behaviour for libtool to try to use only PIC objects.
              The user may still override this default by specifying --without-pic to
              configure.

'no-pic'   Change the default behaviour of libtool to try to use only non-PIC
              objects. The user may still override this default by specifying --with-
              pic to configure.

LT_LANG (*language*)   [Macro]
     Enable libtool support for the language given if it has not yet already been en-
     abled. Languages accepted are "C++", "Fortran 77", "Java", "Go", and "Windows
     Resource".

     If Autoconf language support macros such as AC_PROG_CXX are used in your
     configure.ac, Libtool language support will automatically be enabled.

     Conversely using LT_LANG to enable language support for Libtool will automatically
     enable Autoconf language support as well.

     Both of the following examples are therefore valid ways of adding C++ language sup-
     port to Libtool.

         LT_INIT
         LT_LANG([C++])
         LT_INIT
         AC_PROG_CXX

AC_LIBTOOL_DLOPEN   [Macro]
     This macro is deprecated, the 'dlopen' option to LT_INIT should be used instead.

AC_LIBTOOL_WIN32_DLL   [Macro]
     This macro is deprecated, the 'win32-dll' option to LT_INIT should be used instead.

AC_DISABLE_FAST_INSTALL   [Macro]
> This macro is deprecated, the 'disable-fast-install' option to LT_INIT should be
> used instead.

AC_DISABLE_SHARED   [Macro]
AM_DISABLE_SHARED   [Macro]
> Change the default behaviour for LT_INIT to disable shared libraries. The user
> may still override this default by specifying '--enable-shared'. The option
> 'disable-shared' to LT_INIT is a shorthand for this. AM_DISABLE_SHARED is a
> deprecated alias for AC_DISABLE_SHARED.

AC_ENABLE_SHARED   [Macro]
AM_ENABLE_SHARED   [Macro]
> Change the default behaviour for LT_INIT to enable shared libraries. This is the
> default on all systems where Libtool knows how to create shared libraries. The user
> may still override this default by specifying '--disable-shared'. The option 'shared'
> to LT_INIT is a shorthand for this. AM_ENABLE_SHARED is a deprecated alias for AC_
> ENABLE_SHARED.

AC_DISABLE_STATIC   [Macro]
AM_DISABLE_STATIC   [Macro]
> Change the default behaviour for LT_INIT to disable static libraries. The user
> may still override this default by specifying '--enable-static'. The option
> 'disable-static' to LT_INIT is a shorthand for this. AM_DISABLE_STATIC is a
> deprecated alias for AC_DISABLE_STATIC.

AC_ENABLE_STATIC   [Macro]
AM_ENABLE_STATIC   [Macro]
> Change the default behaviour for LT_INIT to enable static libraries. This is the default
> on all systems where shared libraries have been disabled for some reason, and on most
> systems where shared libraries have been enabled. If shared libraries are enabled, the
> user may still override this default by specifying '--disable-static'. The option
> 'static' to LT_INIT is a shorthand for this. AM_ENABLE_STATIC is a deprecated alias
> for AC_ENABLE_STATIC.

The tests in LT_INIT also recognize the following environment variables:

CC   [Variable]
> The C compiler that will be used by the generated libtool. If this is not set, LT_INIT
> will look for gcc or cc.

CFLAGS   [Variable]
> Compiler flags used to generate standard object files. If this is not set, LT_INIT will
> not use any such flags. It affects only the way LT_INIT runs tests, not the produced
> libtool.

CPPFLAGS   [Variable]
> C preprocessor flags. If this is not set, LT_INIT will not use any such flags. It affects
> only the way LT_INIT runs tests, not the produced libtool.

LD   [Variable]

> The system linker to use (if the generated `libtool` requires one). If this is not set, `LT_INIT` will try to find out what is the linker used by `CC`.

LDFLAGS   [Variable]

> The flags to be used by `libtool` when it links a program. If this is not set, `LT_INIT` will not use any such flags. It affects only the way `LT_INIT` runs tests, not the produced `libtool`.

LIBS   [Variable]

> The libraries to be used by `LT_INIT` when it links a program. If this is not set, `LT_INIT` will not use any such flags. It affects only the way `LT_INIT` runs tests, not the produced `libtool`.

NM   [Variable]

> Program to use rather than checking for `nm`.

RANLIB   [Variable]

> Program to use rather than checking for `ranlib`.

LN_S   [Variable]

> A command that creates a link of a program, a soft-link if possible, a hard-link otherwise. `LT_INIT` will check for a suitable program if this variable is not set.

DLLTOOL   [Variable]

> Program to use rather than checking for `dlltool`. Only meaningful for Cygwin/MS-Windows.

OBJDUMP   [Variable]

> Program to use rather than checking for `objdump`. Only meaningful for Cygwin/MS-Windows.

AS   [Variable]

> Program to use rather than checking for `as`. Only used on Cygwin/MS-Windows at the moment.

MANIFEST_TOOL   [Variable]

> Program to use rather than checking for `mt`, the Manifest Tool. Only used on Cygwin/MS-Windows at the moment.

LT_SYS_LIBRARY_PATH   [Variable]

> Libtool has heuristics for the system search path for runtime-loaded libraries. If the guessed default does not match the setup of the host system, this variable can be used to modify that path list, as follows (`LT_SYS_LIBRARY_PATH` is a colon-delimited list like `PATH`):
>
> - `path:` The heuristically determined paths will be appened after the trailing colon;
> - `:path` The heuristically determined paths will be prepended before the leading colon;
> - `path::path` The heuristically determined paths will be inserted between the double colons;

- `path` With no dangling colons, the heuristically determined paths will be ignored entirely.

With 1.3 era libtool, if you wanted to know any details of what libtool had discovered about your architecture and environment, you had to run the script with `--config` and grep through the results. This idiom was supported up to and including 1.5.x era libtool, where it was possible to call the generated libtool script from `configure.ac` as soon as `LT_INIT` had completed. However, one of the features of libtool 1.4 was that the libtool configuration was migrated out of a separate `ltconfig` file, and added to the `LT_INIT` macro (nee `AC_PROG_LIBTOOL`), so the results of the configuration tests were available directly to code in `configure.ac`, rendering the call out to the generated libtool script obsolete.

Starting with libtool 2.0, the multipass generation of the libtool script has been consolidated into a single `config.status` pass, which happens after all the code in `configure.ac` has completed. The implication of this is that the libtool script does not exist during execution of code from `configure.ac`, and so obviously it cannot be called for `--config` details anymore. If you are upgrading projects that used this idiom to libtool 2.0 or newer, you should replace those calls with direct references to the equivalent Autoconf shell variables that are set by the configure time tests before being passed to `config.status` for inclusion in the generated libtool script.

`LT_OUTPUT`   [Macro]

By default, the configured `libtool` script is generated by the call to `AC_OUTPUT` command, and there is rarely any need to use `libtool` from `configure`. However, sometimes it is necessary to run configure time compile and link tests using `libtool`. You can add `LT_OUTPUT` to your `configure.ac` any time after `LT_INIT` and any `LT_LANG` calls; that done, `libtool` will be created by a specially generated `config.lt` file, and available for use in later tests.

Also, when `LT_OUTPUT` is used, for backwards compatibility with Automake regeneration rules, `config.status` will call `config.lt` to regenerate `libtool`, rather than generating the file itself.

When you invoke the `libtoolize` program (see Section 5.5.1 [Invoking libtoolize], page 35), it will tell you where to find a definition of `LT_INIT`. If you use Automake, the `aclocal` program will automatically add `LT_INIT` support to your `configure` script when it sees the invocation of `LT_INIT` in `configure.ac`.

Because of these changes, and the runtime version compatibility checks Libtool now executes, we now advise **against** including a copy of `libtool.m4` (and brethren) in `acinclude.m4`. Instead, you should set your project macro directory with `AC_CONFIG_MACRO_DIRS`. When you `libtoolize` your project, a copy of the relevant macro definitions will be placed in your `AC_CONFIG_MACRO_DIRS`, where `aclocal` can reference them directly from `aclocal.m4`.

5.4.2 Platform-specific configuration notes

While Libtool tries to hide as many platform-specific features as possible, some have to be taken into account when configuring either the Libtool package or a libtoolized package.

- You currently need GNU make to build the Libtool package itself.

- On AIX there are two different styles of shared linking, one where symbols are bound at link-time and one where symbols are bound at runtime only, similar to ELF. In case of doubt use `LDFLAGS=-Wl,-brtl` for the latter style.

- On AIX, native tools are to be preferred over binutils; especially for C++ code, if using the AIX Toolbox GCC 4.0 and binutils, configure with `AR=/usr/bin/ar LD=/usr/bin/ld NM='/usr/bin/nm -B'`.

- On AIX, the `/bin/sh` is very slow due to its inefficient handling of here-documents. A modern shell is preferable:

      CONFIG_SHELL=/bin/bash; export $CONFIG_SHELL
      $CONFIG_SHELL ./configure [...]

- For C++ code with templates, it may be necessary to specify the way the compiler will generate the instantiations. For Portland pgCC version5, use `CXX='pgCC --one_instantiation_per_object'` and avoid parallel `make`.

- On Darwin, for C++ code with templates you need two level shared libraries. Libtool builds these by default if `MACOSX_DEPLOYMENT_TARGET` is set to 10.3 or later at `configure` time. See `rdar://problem/4135857` for more information on this issue.

- The default shell on UNICOS 9, a ksh 88u variant, is too buggy to correctly execute the libtool script. Users are advised to install a modern shell such as GNU bash.

- Some HP-UX `sed` programs are horribly broken, and cannot handle libtool's requirements, so users may report unusual problems. There is no workaround except to install a working `sed` (such as GNU sed) on these systems.

- The vendor-distributed NCR MP-RAS `cc` programs emits copyright on standard error that confuse tests on size of `conftest.err`. The workaround is to specify `CC` when run configure with `CC='cc -Hnocopyr'`.

- Any earlier DG/UX system with ELF executables, such as R3.10 or R4.10, is also likely to work, but hasn't been explicitly tested.

- On Reliant Unix libtool has only been tested with the Siemens C-compiler and an old version of `gcc` provided by Marco Walther.

- `libtool.m4`, `ltdl.m4` and the `configure.ac` files are marked to use autoconf-mode, which is distributed with GNU Emacs 21, Autoconf itself, and all recent releases of XEmacs.

- When building on some GNU/Linux systems for multilib targets `libtool` sometimes guesses the wrong paths that the linker and dynamic linker search by default. If this occurs for the dynamic library path, you may use the `LT_SYS_LIBRARY_PATH` environment variable to adjust. Otherwise, at `configure` time you may override libtool's guesses by setting the `autoconf` cache variables `lt_cv_sys_lib_search_path_spec` and `lt_cv_sys_lib_dlsearch_path_spec` respectively.

5.5 Including libtool in your package

In order to use libtool, you need to include the following files with your package:

`config.guess`
>Attempt to guess a canonical system name.

config.sub
> Canonical system name validation subroutine script.

install-sh
> BSD-compatible `install` replacement script.

ltmain.sh
> A generic script implementing basic libtool functionality.

Note that the libtool script itself should *not* be included with your package. See Section 5.4 [Configuring], page 27.

You should use the `libtoolize` program, rather than manually copying these files into your package.

5.5.1 Invoking `libtoolize`

The `libtoolize` program provides a standard way to add libtool support to your package. In the future, it may implement better usage checking, or other features to make libtool even easier to use.

The `libtoolize` program has the following synopsis:

    libtoolize [option]...

and accepts the following options:

--copy
-c   Copy files from the libtool data directory rather than creating symlinks.

--debug   Dump a trace of shell script execution to standard output. This produces a lot of output, so you may wish to pipe it to `less` (or `more`) or redirect to a file.

--dry-run
-n   Don't run any commands that modify the file system, just print them out.

--force
-f   Replace existing libtool files. By default, `libtoolize` won't overwrite existing files.

--help   Display a help message and exit.

--ltdl [target-directory-name]
> Install libltdl in the *target-directory-name* subdirectory of your package. Normally, the directory is extracted from the argument to `LT_CONFIG_LTDL_DIR` in `configure.ac`, though you can also specify a subdirectory name here if you are not using Autoconf for example. If `libtoolize` can't determine the target directory, 'libltdl' is used as the default.

--no-warn
> Normally, Libtoolize tries to diagnose use of deprecated libtool macros and other stylistic issues. If you are deliberately using outdated calling conventions, this option prevents Libtoolize from explaining how to update your project's Libtool conventions.

--nonrecursive
> If passed in conjunction with --ltdl, this option will cause the libltdl installed by 'libtoolize' to be set up for use with a non-recursive automake

build. To make use of it, you will need to add the following to the `Makefile.am`
of the parent project:

```
## libltdl/ltdl.mk appends to the following variables
## so we set them here before including it:
BUILT_SOURCES    =

AM_CPPFLAGS        =
AM_LDFLAGS         =

include_HEADERS    =
noinst_LTLIBRARIES =
lib_LTLIBRARIES    =
EXTRA_LTLIBRARIES  =

EXTRA_DIST    =

CLEANFILES    =
MOSTLYCLEANFILES    =

include libltdl/ltdl.mk
```

`--quiet`

`-q`   Work silently. 'libtoolize --quiet' is used by GNU Automake to add libtool
              files to your package if necessary.

`--recursive`

              If passed in conjunction with `--ltdl`, this option will cause the `libtoolize`
              installed 'libltdl' to be set up for use with a recursive `automake` build. To
              make use of it, you will need to adjust the parent project's `configure.ac`:

                     `AC_CONFIG_FILES([libltdl/Makefile])`

              and `Makefile.am`:

                     `SUBDIRS += libltdl`

`--subproject`

              If passed in conjunction with `--ltdl`, this option will cause the `libtoolize`
              installed 'libltdl' to be set up for independent configuration and compilation
              as a self-contained subproject. To make use of it, you should arrange for your
              build to call `libltdl/configure`, and then run `make` in the `libltdl` directory
              (or the subdirectory you put libltdl into). If your project uses Autoconf, you
              can use the supplied 'LT_WITH_LTDL' macro, or else call 'AC_CONFIG_SUBDIRS'
              directly.

              Previous releases of 'libltdl' built exclusively in this mode, but now it is the
              default mode both for backwards compatibility and because, for example, it is
              suitable for use in projects that wish to use 'libltdl', but not use the Autotools
              for their own build process.

`--verbose`

`-v`   Work noisily! Give a blow by blow account of what `libtoolize` is doing.

```
--version
```
        Print `libtoolize` version information and exit.

Sometimes it can be useful to pass options to `libtoolize` even though it is called by another program, such as `autoreconf`. A limited number of options are parsed from the environment variable `LIBTOOLIZE_OPTIONS`: currently `--debug`, `--no-warn`, `--quiet` and `--verbose`. Multiple options passed in `LIBTOOLIZE_OPTIONS` must be separated with a space, comma or a colon.

By default, a warning is issued for unknown options found in `LIBTOOLIZE_OPTIONS` unless the first such option is `--no-warn`. Where `libtoolize` has always quit on receipt of an unknown option at the command line, this and all previous releases of `libtoolize` will continue unabated whatever the content of `LIBTOOLIZE_OPTIONS` (modulo some possible warning messages).

```
trick$ LIBTOOLIZE_OPTIONS=--no-warn,--quiet autoreconf --install
```

If `libtoolize` detects an explicit call to `AC_CONFIG_MACRO_DIRS` (see Section "The Autoconf Manual" in *The Autoconf Manual*) in your `configure.ac`, it will put the Libtool macros in the specified directory.

In the future other Autotools will automatically check the contents of `AC_CONFIG_MACRO_DIRS`, but at the moment it is more portable to add the macro directory to `ACLOCAL_AMFLAGS` in `Makefile.am`, which is where the tools currently look. If `libtoolize` doesn't see `AC_CONFIG_MACRO_DIRS`, it too will honour the first '-I' argument in `ACLOCAL_AMFLAGS` when choosing a directory to store libtool configuration macros in. It is perfectly sensible to use both `AC_CONFIG_MACRO_DIRS` and `ACLOCAL_AMFLAGS`, as long as they are kept in synchronisation.

```
ACLOCAL_AMFLAGS = -I m4
```

When you bootstrap your project with `aclocal`, then you will need to explicitly pass the same macro directory with `aclocal`'s '-I' flag:

```
trick$ aclocal -I m4
```

If `libtoolize` detects an explicit call to `AC_CONFIG_AUX_DIR` (see Section "The Autoconf Manual" in *The Autoconf Manual*) in your `configure.ac`, it will put the other support files in the specified directory. Otherwise they too end up in the project root directory.

Unless `--no-warn` is passed, `libtoolize` displays hints for adding libtool support to your package, as well.

5.5.2 Autoconf and `LTLIBOBJS`

People used to add code like the following to their `configure.ac`:

```
LTLIBOBJS=`echo "$LIBOBJS" | sed 's/\.[^.]* /.lo /g;s/\.[^.]*$/.lo/'`
AC_SUBST([LTLIBOBJS])
```

This is no longer required (since Autoconf 2.54), and doesn't take Automake's deansification support into account either, so doesn't work correctly even with ancient Autoconfs!

Provided you are using a recent (2.54 or better) incarnation of Autoconf, the call to `AC_OUTPUT` takes care of setting `LTLIBOBJS` up correctly, so you can simply delete such snippets from your `configure.ac` if you had them.

5.6 Static-only libraries

When you are developing a package, it is often worthwhile to configure your package
with the `--disable-shared` flag, or to override the defaults for `LT_INIT` by using the
`disable-shared` option (see Section 5.4.1 [The `LT_INIT` macro], page 27). This prevents
libtool from building shared libraries, which has several advantages:

- compilation is twice as fast, which can speed up your development cycle,
- debugging is easier because you don't need to deal with any complexities added by
  shared libraries, and
- you can see how libtool behaves on static-only platforms.

You may want to put a small note in your package `README` to let other developers know
that `--disable-shared` can save them time. The following example note is taken from the
GIMP[3] distribution `README`:

```
The GIMP uses GNU Libtool to build shared libraries on a
variety of systems.  While this is very nice for making usable
binaries, it can be a pain when trying to debug a program.  For that
reason, compilation of shared libraries can be turned off by
specifying the --disable-shared option to configure.
```

---

[3] GNU Image Manipulation Program, for those who haven't taken the plunge. See `http://www.gimp.org/`.

6 Using libtool with other languages

Libtool was first implemented to add support for writing shared libraries in the C language. However, over time, libtool is being integrated with other languages, so that programmers are free to reap the benefits of shared libraries in their favorite programming language.

This chapter describes how libtool interacts with other languages, and what special considerations you need to make if you do not use C.

6.1 Writing libraries for C++

Creating libraries of C++ code should be a fairly straightforward process, because its object files differ from C ones in only three ways:

1. Because of name mangling, C++ libraries are only usable by the C++ compiler that created them. This decision was made by the designers of C++ to protect users from conflicting implementations of features such as constructors, exception handling, and RTTI.

2. On some systems, the C++ compiler must take special actions for the dynamic linker to run dynamic (i.e., run-time) initializers. This means that we should not call `ld` directly to link such libraries, and we should use the C++ compiler instead.

3. C++ compilers will link some Standard C++ library in by default, but libtool does not know what these libraries are, so it cannot even run the inter-library dependence analyzer to check how to link it in. Therefore, running `ld` to link a C++ program or library is deemed to fail.

Because of these three issues, Libtool has been designed to always use the C++ compiler to compile and link C++ programs and libraries. In some instances the `main()` function of a program must also be compiled with the C++ compiler for static C++ objects to be properly initialized.

6.2 Tags

Libtool supports multiple languages through the use of tags. Technically a tag corresponds to a set of configuration variables associated with a language. These variables tell `libtool` how it should create objects and libraries for each language.

Tags are defined at `configure`-time for each language activated in the package (see `LT_LANG` in Section 5.4.1 [LT_INIT], page 27). Here is the correspondence between language names and tags names.

Language name	Tag name
C	CC
C++	CXX
Java	GCJ
Fortran 77	F77
Fortran	FC
Go	GO
Windows Resource	RC

`libtool` tries to automatically infer what tag to use from the compiler command being used to compile or link. If it can't infer a tag, then it defaults to the configuration for the C language.

The tag can also be specified using `libtool`'s `--tag=tag` option (see Chapter 4 [Invoking libtool], page 15). It is a good idea to do so in `Makefile` rules, because that will allow users to substitute the compiler without relying on `libtool` inference heuristics. When no tag is specified, `libtool` will default to `CC`; this tag always exists.

Finally, the set of tags available in a particular project can be retrieved by tracing for the `LT_SUPPORTED_TAG` macro (see Chapter 12 [Trace interface], page 74).

7 Library interface versions

The most difficult issue introduced by shared libraries is that of creating and resolving runtime dependencies. Dependencies on programs and libraries are often described in terms of a single name, such as `sed`. So, one may say "libtool depends on sed," and that is good enough for most purposes.

However, when an interface changes regularly, we need to be more specific: "Gnus 5.1 requires Emacs 19.28 or above." Here, the description of an interface consists of a name, and a "version number."

Even that sort of description is not accurate enough for some purposes. What if Emacs 20 changes enough to break Gnus 5.1?

The same problem exists in shared libraries: we require a formal version system to describe the sorts of dependencies that programs have on shared libraries, so that the dynamic linker can guarantee that programs are linked only against libraries that provide the interface they require.

7.1 What are library interfaces?

Interfaces for libraries may be any of the following (and more):
- global variables: both names and types
- global functions: argument types and number, return types, and function names
- standard input, standard output, standard error, and file formats
- sockets, pipes, and other inter-process communication protocol formats

Note that static functions do not count as interfaces, because they are not directly available to the user of the library.

7.2 Libtool's versioning system

Libtool has its own formal versioning system. It is not as flexible as some, but it is definitely the simplest of the more powerful versioning systems.

Think of a library as exporting several sets of interfaces, arbitrarily represented by integers. When a program is linked against a library, it may use any subset of those interfaces.

Libtool's description of the interfaces that a program uses is simple: it encodes the least and the greatest interface numbers in the resulting binary (*first-interface*, *last-interface*).

The dynamic linker is guaranteed that if a library supports *every* interface number between *first-interface* and *last-interface*, then the program can be relinked against that library.

Note that this can cause problems because libtool's compatibility requirements are actually stricter than is necessary.

Say `libhello` supports interfaces 5, 16, 17, 18, and 19, and that libtool is used to link `test` against `libhello`.

Libtool encodes the numbers 5 and 19 in `test`, and the dynamic linker will only link `test` against libraries that support *every* interface between 5 and 19. So, the dynamic linker refuses to link `test` against `libhello`!

In order to eliminate this problem, libtool only allows libraries to declare consecutive interface numbers. So, `libhello` can declare at most that it supports interfaces 16 through 19. Then, the dynamic linker will link `test` against `libhello`.

So, libtool library versions are described by three integers:

current   The most recent interface number that this library implements.

revision   The implementation number of the *current* interface.

age   The difference between the newest and oldest interfaces that this library implements. In other words, the library implements all the interface numbers in the range from number `current - age` to `current`.

If two libraries have identical *current* and *age* numbers, then the dynamic linker chooses the library with the greater *revision* number.

7.3 Updating library version information

If you want to use libtool's versioning system, then you must specify the version information to libtool using the `-version-info` flag during link mode (see Section 4.2 [Link mode], page 18).

This flag accepts an argument of the form '*current*[:*revision*[:*age*]]'. So, passing `-version-info 3:12:1` sets *current* to 3, *revision* to 12, and *age* to 1.

If either *revision* or *age* are omitted, they default to 0. Also note that *age* must be less than or equal to the *current* interface number.

Here are a set of rules to help you update your library version information:

1. Start with version information of '`0:0:0`' for each libtool library.

2. Update the version information only immediately before a public release of your software. More frequent updates are unnecessary, and only guarantee that the current interface number gets larger faster.

3. If the library source code has changed at all since the last update, then increment *revision* ('`c:r:a`' becomes '`c:r + 1:a`').

4. If any interfaces have been added, removed, or changed since the last update, increment *current*, and set *revision* to 0.

5. If any interfaces have been added since the last public release, then increment *age*.

6. If any interfaces have been removed or changed since the last public release, then set *age* to 0.

Never try to set the interface numbers so that they correspond to the release number of your package. This is an abuse that only fosters misunderstanding of the purpose of library versions. Instead, use the `-release` flag (see Section 7.4 [Release numbers], page 43), but be warned that every release of your package will not be binary compatible with any other release.

The following explanation may help to understand the above rules a bit better: consider that there are three possible kinds of reactions from users of your library to changes in a shared library:

1. Programs using the previous version may use the new version as drop-in replacement, and programs using the new version can also work with the previous one. In other words, no recompiling nor relinking is needed. In this case, bump *revision* only, don't touch *current* nor *age*.

2. Programs using the previous version may use the new version as drop-in replacement, but programs using the new version may use APIs not present in the previous one. In other words, a program linking against the new version may fail with "unresolved symbols" if linking against the old version at runtime: set *revision* to 0, bump *current* and *age*.

3. Programs may need to be changed, recompiled, and relinked in order to use the new version. Bump *current*, set *revision* and *age* to 0.

In the above description, *programs* using the library in question may also be replaced by other libraries using it.

7.4 Managing release information

Often, people want to encode the name of the package release into the shared library so that it is obvious to the user what package their programs are linked against. This convention is used especially on GNU/Linux:

```
trick$ ls /usr/lib/libbfd*
/usr/lib/libbfd.a            /usr/lib/libbfd.so.2.7.0.2
/usr/lib/libbfd.so
trick$
```

On 'trick', /usr/lib/libbfd.so is a symbolic link to libbfd.so.2.7.0.2, which was distributed as a part of 'binutils-2.7.0.2'.

Unfortunately, this convention conflicts directly with libtool's idea of library interface versions, because the library interface rarely changes at the same time that the release number does, and the library suffix is never the same across all platforms.

So, to accommodate both views, you can use the -release flag to set release information for libraries for which you do not want to use -version-info. For the libbfd example, the next release that uses libtool should be built with '-release 2.9.0', which will produce the following files on GNU/Linux:

```
trick$ ls /usr/lib/libbfd*
/usr/lib/libbfd-2.9.0.so    /usr/lib/libbfd.a
/usr/lib/libbfd.so
trick$
```

In this case, /usr/lib/libbfd.so is a symbolic link to libbfd-2.9.0.so. This makes it obvious that the user is dealing with 'binutils-2.9.0', without compromising libtool's idea of interface versions.

Note that this option causes a modification of the library name, so do not use it unless you want to break binary compatibility with any past library releases. In general, you should only use -release for package-internal libraries or for ones whose interfaces change very frequently.

8 Tips for interface design

Writing a good library interface takes a lot of practice and thorough understanding of the problem that the library is intended to solve.

If you design a good interface, it won't have to change often, you won't have to keep updating documentation, and users won't have to keep relearning how to use the library.

Here is a brief list of tips for library interface design that may help you in your exploits:

Plan ahead
> Try to make every interface truly minimal, so that you won't need to delete entry points very often.

Avoid interface changes
> Some people love redesigning and changing entry points just for the heck of it (note: *renaming* a function is considered changing an entry point). Don't be one of those people. If you must redesign an interface, then try to leave compatibility functions behind so that users don't need to rewrite their existing code.

Use opaque data types
> The fewer data type definitions a library user has access to, the better. If possible, design your functions to accept a generic pointer (that you can cast to an internal data type), and provide access functions rather than allowing the library user to directly manipulate the data. That way, you have the freedom to change the data structures without changing the interface.
>
> This is essentially the same thing as using abstract data types and inheritance in an object-oriented system.

Use header files
> If you are careful to document each of your library's global functions and variables in header files, and include them in your library source files, then the compiler will let you know if you make any interface changes by accident (see Section 8.1 [C header files], page 45).

Use the `static` keyword (or equivalent) whenever possible
> The fewer global functions your library has, the more flexibility you'll have in changing them. Static functions and variables may change forms as often as you like... your users cannot access them, so they aren't interface changes.

Be careful with array dimensions
> The number of elements in a global array is part of an interface, even if the header just declares `extern int foo[];`. This is because on i386 and some other SVR4/ELF systems, when an application references data in a shared library the size of that data (whatever its type) is included in the application executable. If you might want to change the size of an array or string then provide a pointer not the actual array.

8.1 Writing C header files

Writing portable C header files can be difficult, since they may be read by different types of compilers:

C++ compilers

> C++ compilers require that functions be declared with full prototypes, since C++ is more strongly typed than C. C functions and variables also need to be declared with the `extern "C"` directive, so that the names aren't mangled. See Section 6.1 [C++ libraries], page 39, for other issues relevant to using C++ with libtool.

ANSI C compilers

> ANSI C compilers are not as strict as C++ compilers, but functions should be prototyped to avoid unnecessary warnings when the header file is `#include`d.

non-ANSI C compilers

> Non-ANSI compilers will report errors if functions are prototyped.

These complications mean that your library interface headers must use some C preprocessor magic to be usable by each of the above compilers.

`foo.h` in the `tests/demo` subdirectory of the libtool distribution serves as an example for how to write a header file that can be safely installed in a system directory.

Here are the relevant portions of that file:

```
/* BEGIN_C_DECLS should be used at the beginning of your declarations,
   so that C++ compilers don't mangle their names.  Use END_C_DECLS at
   the end of C declarations. */
#undef BEGIN_C_DECLS
#undef END_C_DECLS
#ifdef __cplusplus
# define BEGIN_C_DECLS extern "C" {
# define END_C_DECLS }
#else
# define BEGIN_C_DECLS /* empty */
# define END_C_DECLS /* empty */
#endif


/* PARAMS is a macro used to wrap function prototypes, so that
   compilers that don't understand ANSI C prototypes still work,
   and ANSI C compilers can issue warnings about type mismatches. */
#undef PARAMS
#if defined __STDC__ || defined _AIX \
        || (defined __mips && defined _SYSTYPE_SVR4) \
        || defined WIN32 || defined __cplusplus
# define PARAMS(protos) protos
#else
# define PARAMS(protos) ()
#endif
```

These macros are used in `foo.h` as follows:

```
#ifndef FOO_H
#define FOO_H 1

/* The above macro definitions. */
#include "..."

BEGIN_C_DECLS

int foo PARAMS((void));
int hello PARAMS((void));

END_C_DECLS

#endif /* !FOO_H */
```

Note that the `#ifndef FOO_H` prevents the body of `foo.h` from being read more than once in a given compilation.

Also the only thing that must go outside the `BEGIN_C_DECLS`/`END_C_DECLS` pair are `#include` lines. Strictly speaking it is only C symbol names that need to be protected, but your header files will be more maintainable if you have a single pair of these macros around the majority of the header contents.

You should use these definitions of `PARAMS`, `BEGIN_C_DECLS`, and `END_C_DECLS` into your own headers. Then, you may use them to create header files that are valid for C++, ANSI, and non-ANSI compilers[1].

Do not be naive about writing portable code. Following the tips given above will help you miss the most obvious problems, but there are definitely other subtle portability issues. You may need to cope with some of the following issues:

- Pre-ANSI compilers do not always support the **void** * generic pointer type, and so need to use **char** * in its place.

- The **const**, **inline** and **signed** keywords are not supported by some compilers, especially pre-ANSI compilers.

- The **long double** type is not supported by many compilers.

---

[1] We used to recommend `__P`, `__BEGIN_DECLS` and `__END_DECLS`. This was bad advice since symbols (even preprocessor macro names) that begin with an underscore are reserved for the use of the compiler.

9 Inter-library dependencies

By definition, every shared library system provides a way for executables to depend on libraries, so that symbol resolution is deferred until runtime.

An *inter-library dependency* is where a library depends on other libraries. For example, if the libtool library `libhello` uses the `cos` function, then it has an inter-library dependency on `libm`, the math library that implements `cos`.

Some shared library systems provide this feature in an internally-consistent way: these systems allow chains of dependencies of potentially infinite length.

However, most shared library systems are restricted in that they only allow a single level of dependencies. In these systems, programs may depend on shared libraries, but shared libraries may not depend on other shared libraries.

In any event, libtool provides a simple mechanism for you to declare inter-library dependencies: for every library `libname` that your own library depends on, simply add a corresponding `-lname` option to the link line when you create your library. To make an example of our `libhello` that depends on `libm`:

```
burger$ libtool --mode=link gcc -g -O -o libhello.la foo.lo hello.lo \
                -rpath /usr/local/lib -lm
burger$
```

When you link a program against `libhello`, you don't need to specify the same '-l' options again: libtool will do that for you, to guarantee that all the required libraries are found. This restriction is only necessary to preserve compatibility with static library systems and simple dynamic library systems.

Some platforms, such as Windows, do not even allow you this flexibility. In order to build a shared library, it must be entirely self-contained or it must have dependencies known at link time (that is, have references only to symbols that are found in the `.lo` files or the specified '-l' libraries), and you need to specify the `-no-undefined` flag. By default, libtool builds only static libraries on these kinds of platforms.

The simple-minded inter-library dependency tracking code of libtool releases prior to 1.2 was disabled because it was not clear when it was possible to link one library with another, and complex failures would occur. A more complex implementation of this concept was re-introduced before release 1.3, but it has not been ported to all platforms that libtool supports. The default, conservative behavior is to avoid linking one library with another, introducing their inter-dependencies only when a program is linked with them.

10 Dlopened modules

It can sometimes be confusing to discuss *dynamic linking*, because the term is used to refer to two different concepts:

1. Compiling and linking a program against a shared library, which is resolved automatically at run time by the dynamic linker. In this process, dynamic linking is transparent to the application.

2. The application calling functions such as `dlopen` that load arbitrary, user-specified modules at runtime. This type of dynamic linking is explicitly controlled by the application.

To mitigate confusion, this manual refers to the second type of dynamic linking as *dlopening* a module.

The main benefit to dlopening object modules is the ability to access compiled object code to extend your program, rather than using an interpreted language. In fact, dlopen calls are frequently used in language interpreters to provide an efficient way to extend the language.

Libtool provides support for dlopened modules. However, you should indicate that your package is willing to use such support, by using the `LT_INIT` option 'dlopen' in `configure.ac`. If this option is not given, libtool will assume no dlopening mechanism is available, and will try to simulate it.

This chapter discusses how you as a dlopen application developer might use libtool to generate dlopen-accessible modules.

10.1 Building modules to dlopen

On some operating systems, a program symbol must be specially declared in order to be dynamically resolved with the `dlsym` (or equivalent) function. Libtool provides the `-export-dynamic` and `-module` link flags (see Section 4.2 [Link mode], page 18), for you to make that declaration. You need to use these flags if you are linking an application program that dlopens other modules or a libtool library that will also be dlopened.

For example, if we wanted to build a shared library, `hello`, that would later be dlopened by an application, we would add `-module` to the other link flags:

```
burger$ libtool --mode=link gcc -module -o hello.la foo.lo \
                hello.lo -rpath /usr/local/lib -lm
burger$
```

If symbols from your *executable* are needed to satisfy unresolved references in a library you want to dlopen you will have to use the flag `-export-dynamic`. You should use `-export-dynamic` while linking the executable that calls dlopen:

```
burger$ libtool --mode=link gcc -export-dynamic -o helldl main.o
burger$
```

10.2 Dlpreopening

Libtool provides special support for dlopening libtool object and libtool library files, so that their symbols can be resolved *even on platforms without any* dlopen *and* dlsym *functions*.

Consider the following alternative ways of loading code into your program, in order of increasing "laziness":

1. Linking against object files that become part of the program executable, whether or not they are referenced. If an object file cannot be found, then the compile time linker refuses to create the executable.

2. Declaring a static library to the linker, so that it is searched at link time to satisfy any undefined references in the above object files. If the static library cannot be found, then the compile time linker refuses to create the executable.

3. Declaring a shared library to the runtime linker, so that it is searched at runtime to satisfy any undefined references in the above files. If the shared library cannot be found, then the dynamic linker aborts the program before it runs.

4. Dlopening a module, so that the application can resolve its own, dynamically-computed references. If there is an error opening the module, or the module is not found, then the application can recover without crashing.

Libtool emulates -dlopen on static platforms by linking objects into the program at compile time, and creating data structures that represent the program's symbol table. In order to use this feature, you must declare the objects you want your application to dlopen by using the -dlopen or -dlpreopen flags when you link your program (see Section 4.2 [Link mode], page 18).

lt_dlsymlist *typedef struct { const char* **name**; *void* **address**; *}*   [Data Type]
        lt_dlsymlist

    The *name* attribute is a null-terminated character string of the symbol name, such as "fprintf". The *address* attribute is a generic pointer to the appropriate object, such as &fprintf.

const lt_dlsymlist lt_preloaded_symbols[]   [Variable]

    An array of lt_dlsymlist structures, representing all the preloaded symbols linked into the program proper. For each module -dlpreopened by the Libtool linked program there is an element with the *name* of the module and an *address* of 0, followed by all symbols exported from this file. For the executable itself the special name '@PROGRAM@' is used. The last element of all has a *name* and *address* of 0.

    To facilitate inclusion of symbol lists into libraries, lt_preloaded_symbols is '#define'd to a suitably unique name in ltdl.h.

    This variable may not be declared const on some systems due to relocation issues.

Some compilers may allow identifiers that are not valid in ANSI C, such as dollar signs. Libtool only recognizes valid ANSI C symbols (an initial ASCII letter or underscore, followed by zero or more ASCII letters, digits, and underscores), so non-ANSI symbols will not appear in lt_preloaded_symbols.

int **lt_dlpreload** (*const lt_dlsymlist *preloaded*)   [Function]
> Register the list of preloaded modules *preloaded*. If *preloaded* is NULL, then all pre-
> viously registered symbol lists, except the list set by **lt_dlpreload_default**, are
> deleted. Return 0 on success.

int **lt_dlpreload_default** (*const lt_dlsymlist *preloaded*)   [Function]
> Set the default list of preloaded modules to *preloaded*, which won't be deleted by
> **lt_dlpreload**. Note that this function does *not* require libltdl to be initialized using
> **lt_dlinit** and can be used in the program to register the default preloaded modules.
> Instead of calling this function directly, most programs will use the macro LTDL_SET_
> PRELOADED_SYMBOLS.
>
> Return 0 on success.

LTDL_SET_PRELOADED_SYMBOLS   [Macro]
> Set the default list of preloaded symbols. Should be used in your program to initialize
> libltdl's list of preloaded modules.
>
> ```
> #include <ltdl.h>
>
> int main() {
>   /* ... */
>   LTDL_SET_PRELOADED_SYMBOLS();
>   /* ... */
> }
> ```

int **lt_dlpreload_callback_func** (*lt_dlhandle handle*)   [Function Type]
> Functions of this type can be passed to **lt_dlpreload_open**, which in turn will call
> back into a function thus passed for each preloaded module that it opens.

int **lt_dlpreload_open** (*const char *originator*,   [Function]
>   *lt_dlpreload_callback_func *func*)
> Load all of the preloaded modules for *originator*. For every module opened in this
> way, call *func*.
>
> To open all of the modules preloaded into libhell.la (presumably from within the
> libhell.a initialisation code):
>
> ```
> #define preloaded_symbols lt_libhell_LTX_preloaded_symbols
>
> static int hell_preload_callback (lt_dlhandle handle);
>
> int
> hell_init (void)
> {
>   ...
>   if (lt_dlpreload (&preloaded_symbols) == 0)
>     {
>       lt_dlpreload_open ("libhell", preload_callback);
>     }
>   ...
> ```

```
        }
```

Note that to prevent clashes between multiple preloaded modules, the preloaded symbols are accessed via a mangled symbol name: to get the symbols preloaded into 'libhell', you must prefix 'preloaded_symbols' with 'lt_'; the originator name, 'libhell' in this case; and '_LTX_'. That is, 'lt_libhell_LTX_preloaded_symbols' here.

10.3 Linking with dlopened modules

When, say, an interpreter application uses dlopened modules to extend the list of methods it provides, an obvious abstraction for the maintainers of the interpreter is to have all methods (including the built in ones supplied with the interpreter) accessed through dlopen. For one thing, the dlopening functionality will be tested even during routine invocations. For another, only one subsystem has to be written for getting methods into the interpreter.

The downside of this abstraction is, of course, that environments that provide only static linkage can't even load the intrinsic interpreter methods. Not so! We can statically link those methods by **dlpreopening** them.

Unfortunately, since platforms such as AIX and cygwin require that all library symbols must be resolved at compile time, the interpreter maintainers will need to provide a library to both its own dlpreopened modules, and third-party modules loaded by dlopen. In itself, that is not so bad, except that the interpreter too must provide those same symbols otherwise it will be impossible to resolve all the symbols required by the modules as they are loaded. Things are even worse if the code that loads the modules for the interpreter is itself in a library – and that is usually the case for any non-trivial application. Modern platforms take care of this by automatically loading all of a module's dependency libraries as the module is loaded (libltdl can do this even on platforms that can't do it by themselves). In the end, this leads to problems with duplicated symbols and prevents modules from loading, and prevents the application from compiling when modules are preloaded.

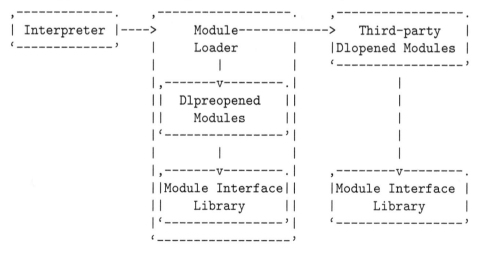

Libtool has the concept of *weak library interfaces* to circumvent this problem. Recall that the code that dlopens method-provider modules for the interpreter application resides in a library: All of the modules and the dlopener library itself should be linked against the common library that resolves the module symbols at compile time. To guard against duplicate symbol definitions, and for dlpreopened modules to work at all in this scenario, the dlopener library must declare that it provides a weak library interface to the common symbols in the library it shares with the modules. That way, when `libtool` links the **Module Loader** library with some **Dlpreopened Modules** that were in turn linked against the **Module Interface Library**, it knows that the **Module Loader** provides an already loaded **Module Interface Library** to resolve symbols for the **Dlpreopened Modules**, and doesn't ask the compiler driver to link an identical **Module Interface Library** dependency library too.

In conjunction with Automake, the `Makefile.am` for the **Module Loader** might look like this:

```
lib_LTLIBRARIES = libinterface.la libloader.la

libinterface_la_SOURCES = interface.c interface.h
libinterface_la_LDFLAGS = -version-info 3:2:1

libloader_la_SOURCES    = loader.c
libloader_la_LDFLAGS    = -weak libinterface.la \
                          -version-info 3:2:1 \
                          -dlpreopen ../modules/intrinsics.la
libloader_la_LIBADD     = $(libinterface_la_OBJECTS)
```

And the `Makefile.am` for the `intrinsics.la` module in a sibling `modules` directory might look like this:

```
AM_CPPFLAGS             = -I$(srcdir)/../libloader
AM_LDFLAGS              = -no-undefined -module -avoid-version \
                          -export-dynamic

noinst_LTLIBRARIES      = intrinsics.la

intrinsics_la_LIBADD    = ../libloader/libinterface.la

../libloader/libinterface.la:
        cd ../libloader && $(MAKE) $(AM_MAKEFLAGS) libinterface.la
```

For a more complex example, see the sources of `libltdl` in the Libtool distribution, which is built with the help of the `-weak` option.

10.4 Finding the correct name to dlopen

After a library has been linked with `-module`, it can be dlopened. Unfortunately, because of the variation in library names, your package needs to determine the correct file to dlopen.

The most straightforward and flexible implementation is to determine the name at run-time, by finding the installed `.la` file, and searching it for the following lines:

```
# The name that we can dlopen.
dlname='dlname'
```

If *dlname* is empty, then the library cannot be dlopened. Otherwise, it gives the dlname of the library. So, if the library was installed as `/usr/local/lib/libhello.la`, and the *dlname* was `libhello.so.3`, then `/usr/local/lib/libhello.so.3` should be dlopened.

If your program uses this approach, then it should search the directories listed in the LD_
LIBRARY_PATH[1] environment variable, as well as the directory where libraries will eventually
be installed. Searching this variable (or equivalent) will guarantee that your program can
find its dlopened modules, even before installation, provided you have linked them using
libtool.

10.5 Unresolved dlopen issues

The following problems are not solved by using libtool's dlopen support:

- Dlopen functions are generally only available on shared library platforms. If you want
  your package to be portable to static platforms, you have to use either libltdl (see
  Chapter 11 [Using libltdl], page 54) or develop your own alternatives to dlopening
  dynamic code. Most reasonable solutions involve writing wrapper functions for the
  dlopen family, which do package-specific tricks when dlopening is unsupported or not
  available on a given platform.

- There are major differences in implementations of the dlopen family of functions. Some
  platforms do not even use the same function names (notably HP-UX, with its shl_load
  family).

- The application developer must write a custom search function to discover the correct
  module filename to supply to dlopen.

---

[1] LIBPATH on AIX, and SHLIB_PATH on HP-UX.

11 Using libltdl

Libtool provides a small library, called `libltdl`, that aims at hiding the various difficulties of dlopening libraries from programmers. It consists of a few headers and small C source files that can be distributed with applications that need dlopening functionality. On some platforms, whose dynamic linkers are too limited for a simple implementation of `libltdl` services, it requires GNU DLD, or it will only emulate dynamic linking with libtool's dlpre-opening mechanism.

libltdl supports currently the following dynamic linking mechanisms:

- `dlopen` (POSIX compliant systems, GNU/Linux, etc.)
- `shl_load` (HP-UX)
- `LoadLibrary` (Win16 and Win32)
- `load_add_on` (BeOS)
- `NSAddImage` or `NSLinkModule` (Darwin and Mac OS X)
- GNU DLD (emulates dynamic linking for static libraries)
- libtool's dlpreopen (see Section 10.2 [Dlpreopening], page 49)

libltdl is licensed under the terms of the GNU Lesser General Public License, with the following exception:

> As a special exception to the GNU Lesser General Public License, if you distribute this file as part of a program or library that is built using GNU Libtool, you may include it under the same distribution terms that you use for the rest of that program.

11.1 How to use libltdl in your programs

The libltdl API is similar to the POSIX dlopen interface, which is very simple but powerful.

To use libltdl in your program you have to include the header file `ltdl.h`:

```
#include <ltdl.h>
```

The early releases of libltdl used some symbols that violated the POSIX namespace conventions. These symbols are now deprecated, and have been replaced by those described here. If you have code that relies on the old deprecated symbol names, defining 'LT_NON_POSIX_NAMESPACE' before you include `ltdl.h` provides conversion macros. Whichever set of symbols you use, the new API is not binary compatible with the last, so you will need to recompile your application to use this version of libltdl.

Note that libltdl is not well tested in a multithreaded environment, though the intention is that it should work (see Section 11.3 [Using libltdl in a multi threaded environment], page 61). It was reported that GNU/Linux's glibc 2.0's `dlopen` with 'RTLD_LAZY' (that libltdl uses by default) is not thread-safe, but this problem is supposed to be fixed in glibc 2.1. On the other hand, 'RTLD_NOW' was reported to introduce problems in multi-threaded applications on FreeBSD. Working around these problems is left as an exercise for the reader; contributions are certainly welcome.

The following macros are defined by including `ltdl.h`:

LT_PATHSEP_CHAR   [Macro]

>   `LT_PATHSEP_CHAR` is the system-dependent path separator, that is, ';' on Windows
>   and ':' everywhere else.

LT_DIRSEP_CHAR   [Macro]

>   If `LT_DIRSEP_CHAR` is defined, it can be used as directory separator in addition to '/'.
>   On Windows, this contains '\'.

The following types are defined in `ltdl.h`:

lt_dlhandle   [Type]

>   `lt_dlhandle` is a module "handle". Every lt_dlopened module has a handle associ-
>   ated with it.

lt_dladvise   [Type]

>   `lt_dladvise` is used to control optional module loading modes. If it is not used, the
>   default mode of the underlying system module loader is used.

lt_dlsymlist   [Type]

>   `lt_dlsymlist` is a symbol list for dlpreopened modules (see Section 10.2 [Dlpreopen-
>   ing], page 49).

libltdl provides the following functions:

int lt_dlinit (*void*)   [Function]
> Initialize libltdl. This function must be called before using libltdl and may be called several times. Return 0 on success, otherwise the number of errors.

int lt_dlexit (*void*)   [Function]
> Shut down libltdl and close all modules. This function will only then shut down libltdl when it was called as many times as `lt_dlinit` has been successfully called. Return 0 on success, otherwise the number of errors.

lt_dlhandle lt_dlopen (*const char *filename*)   [Function]
> Open the module with the file name *filename* and return a handle for it. `lt_dlopen` is able to open libtool dynamic modules, preloaded static modules, the program itself and native dynamic modules[1].
>
> Unresolved symbols in the module are resolved using its dependency libraries and previously dlopened modules. If the executable using this module was linked with the `-export-dynamic` flag, then the global symbols in the executable will also be used to resolve references in the module.
>
> If *filename* is `NULL` and the program was linked with `-export-dynamic` or `-dlopen self`, `lt_dlopen` will return a handle for the program itself, which can be used to access its symbols.
>
> If libltdl cannot find the library and the file name *filename* does not have a directory component it will additionally look in the following search paths for the module (in the following order):
>
> 1. user-defined search path: This search path can be changed by the program using the functions `lt_dlsetsearchpath`, `lt_dladdsearchdir` and `lt_dlinsertsearchdir`.
>
> 2. libltdl's search path: This search path is the value of the environment variable `LTDL_LIBRARY_PATH`.
>
> 3. system library search path: The system dependent library search path (e.g. on GNU/Linux it is `LD_LIBRARY_PATH`).
>
> Each search path must be a list of absolute directories separated by `LT_PATHSEP_CHAR`, for example, `"/usr/lib/mypkg:/lib/foo"`. The directory names may not contain the path separator.
>
> If the same module is loaded several times, the same handle is returned. If `lt_dlopen` fails for any reason, it returns `NULL`.

lt_dlhandle lt_dlopenext (*const char *filename*)   [Function]
> The same as `lt_dlopen`, except that it tries to append different file name extensions to the file name. If the file with the file name *filename* cannot be found libltdl tries to append the following extensions:
>
> 1. the libtool archive extension `.la`

---

[1] Some platforms, notably Mac OS X, differentiate between a runtime library that cannot be opened by `lt_dlopen` and a dynamic module that can. For maximum portability you should try to ensure that you only pass `lt_dlopen` objects that have been compiled with libtool's `-module` flag.

2. the extension used for native dynamically loadable modules on the host platform, e.g., `.so`, `.sl`, etc.

This lookup strategy was designed to allow programs that don't have knowledge about native dynamic libraries naming conventions to be able to `dlopen` such libraries as well as libtool modules transparently.

`lt_dlhandle lt_dlopenadvise` (*const char* `*filename`,   [Function]
    lt_dladvise `advise`)

The same as `lt_dlopen`, except that it also requires an additional argument that may contain additional hints to the underlying system module loader. The *advise* parameter is opaque and can only be accessed with the functions documented below.

Note that this function does not change the content of *advise*, so unlike the other calls in this API takes a direct `lt_dladvise` type, and not a pointer to the same.

`int lt_dladvise_init` (*lt_dladvise* `*advise`)   [Function]

The *advise* parameter can be used to pass hints to the module loader when using `lt_dlopenadvise` to perform the loading. The *advise* parameter needs to be initialised by this function before it can be used. Any memory used by *advise* needs to be recycled with `lt_dladvise_destroy` when it is no longer needed.

On failure, `lt_dladvise_init` returns non-zero and sets an error message that can be retrieved with `lt_dlerror`.

`int lt_dladvise_destroy` (*lt_dladvise* `*advise`)   [Function]

Recycle the memory used by *advise*. For an example, see the documentation for `lt_dladvise_ext`.

On failure, `lt_dladvise_destroy` returns non-zero and sets an error message that can be retrieved with `lt_dlerror`.

`int lt_dladvise_ext` (*lt_dladvise* `*advise`)   [Function]

Set the `ext` hint on *advise*. Passing an *advise* parameter to `lt_dlopenadvise` with this hint set causes it to try to append different file name extensions like `lt_dlopenext`.

The following example is equivalent to calling `lt_dlopenext (filename)`:

```
lt_dlhandle
my_dlopenext (const char *filename)
{
  lt_dlhandle handle = 0;
  lt_dladvise advise;

  if (!lt_dladvise_init (&advise) && !lt_dladvise_ext (&advise))
    handle = lt_dlopenadvise (filename, advise);

  lt_dladvise_destroy (&advise);

  return handle;
}
```

On failure, `lt_dladvise_ext` returns non-zero and sets an error message that can be retrieved with `lt_dlerror`.

int `lt_dladvise_global` (`lt_dladvise *advise`)   [Function]
> Set the `symglobal` hint on *advise*. Passing an *advise* parameter to `lt_dlopenadvise` with this hint set causes it to try to make the loaded module's symbols globally available for resolving unresolved symbols in subsequently loaded modules.
>
> If neither the `symglobal` nor the `symlocal` hints are set, or if a module is loaded without using the `lt_dlopenadvise` call in any case, then the visibility of the module's symbols will be as per the default for the underlying module loader and OS. Even if a suitable hint is passed, not all loaders are able to act upon it in which case `lt_dlgetinfo` will reveal whether the hint was actually followed.
>
> On failure, `lt_dladvise_global` returns non-zero and sets an error message that can be retrieved with `lt_dlerror`.

int `lt_dladvise_local` (`lt_dladvise *advise`)   [Function]
> Set the `symlocal` hint on *advise*. Passing an *advise* parameter to `lt_dlopenadvise` with this hint set causes it to try to keep the loaded module's symbols hidden so that they are not visible to subsequently loaded modules.
>
> If neither the `symglobal` nor the `symlocal` hints are set, or if a module is loaded without using the `lt_dlopenadvise` call in any case, then the visibility of the module's symbols will be as per the default for the underlying module loader and OS. Even if a suitable hint is passed, not all loaders are able to act upon it in which case `lt_dlgetinfo` will reveal whether the hint was actually followed.
>
> On failure, `lt_dladvise_local` returns non-zero and sets an error message that can be retrieved with `lt_dlerror`.

int `lt_dladvise_resident` (`lt_dladvise *advise`)   [Function]
> Set the `resident` hint on *advise*. Passing an *advise* parameter to `lt_dlopenadvise` with this hint set causes it to try to make the loaded module resident in memory, so that it cannot be unloaded with a later call to `lt_dlclose`.
>
> On failure, `lt_dladvise_resident` returns non-zero and sets an error message that can be retrieved with `lt_dlerror`.

int `lt_dladvise_preload` (`lt_dladvise *advise`)   [Function]
> Set the `preload` hint on *advise*. Passing an *advise* parameter to `lt_dlopenadvise` with this hint set causes it to load only preloaded modules, so that if a suitable preloaded module is not found, `lt_dlopenadvise` will return NULL.

int `lt_dlclose` (`lt_dlhandle handle`)   [Function]
> Decrement the reference count on the module *handle*. If it drops to zero and no other module depends on this module, then the module is unloaded. Return 0 on success.

void * `lt_dlsym` (`lt_dlhandle handle`, `const char *name`)   [Function]
> Return the address in the module *handle*, where the symbol given by the null-terminated string *name* is loaded. If the symbol cannot be found, NULL is returned.

const char * lt_dlerror (*void*) [Function]
> Return a human readable string describing the most recent error that occurred from any of libltdl's functions. Return NULL if no errors have occurred since initialization or since it was last called.

int lt_dladdsearchdir (*const char *search_dir*) [Function]
> Append the search directory *search_dir* to the current user-defined library search path. Return 0 on success.

int lt_dlinsertsearchdir (*const char *before*, [Function]
>   *const char *search_dir*)
> Insert the search directory *search_dir* into the user-defined library search path, immediately before the element starting at address *before*. If *before* is 'NULL', then *search_dir* is appending as if lt_dladdsearchdir had been called. Return 0 on success.

int lt_dlsetsearchpath (*const char *search_path*) [Function]
> Replace the current user-defined library search path with *search_path*, which must be a list of absolute directories separated by LT_PATHSEP_CHAR. Return 0 on success.

const char * lt_dlgetsearchpath (*void*) [Function]
> Return the current user-defined library search path.

int lt_dlforeachfile (*const char *search_path*, [Function]
>   *int (*func) (const char *filename, void * data), void * data*)
> In some applications you may not want to load individual modules with known names, but rather find all of the modules in a set of directories and load them all during initialisation. With this function you can have libltdl scan the LT_PATHSEP_CHAR-delimited directory list in *search_path* for candidates, and pass them, along with *data* to your own callback function, *func*. If *search_path* is 'NULL', then search all of the standard locations that lt_dlopen would examine. This function will continue to make calls to *func* for each file that it discovers in *search_path* until one of these calls returns non-zero, or until the files are exhausted. 'lt_dlforeachfile' returns the value returned by the last call made to *func*.
>
> For example you could define *func* to build an ordered *argv*-like vector of files using *data* to hold the address of the start of the vector.

int lt_dlmakeresident (*lt_dlhandle handle*) [Function]
> Mark a module so that it cannot be 'lt_dlclose'd. This can be useful if a module implements some core functionality in your project that would cause your code to crash if removed. Return 0 on success.
>
> If you use 'lt_dlopen (NULL)' to get a *handle* for the running binary, that handle will always be marked as resident, and consequently cannot be successfully 'lt_dlclose'd.

int lt_dlisresident (*lt_dlhandle handle*) [Function]
> Check whether a particular module has been marked as resident, returning 1 if it has or 0 otherwise. If there is an error while executing this function, return -1 and set an error message for retrieval with lt_dlerror.

11.2 Creating modules that can be `dlopen`ed

Libtool modules are created like normal libtool libraries with a few exceptions:

You have to link the module with libtool's `-module` switch, and you should link any program that is intended to dlopen the module with `-dlopen modulename.la` where possible, so that libtool can dlpreopen the module on platforms that do not support dlopening. If the module depends on any other libraries, make sure you specify them either when you link the module or when you link programs that dlopen it. If you want to disable versioning (see Chapter 7 [Versioning], page 41) for a specific module you should link it with the `-avoid-version` switch. Note that libtool modules don't need to have a "lib" prefix. However, Automake 1.4 or higher is required to build such modules.

Usually a set of modules provide the same interface, i.e. exports the same symbols, so that a program can dlopen them without having to know more about their internals: In order to avoid symbol conflicts all exported symbols must be prefixed with "modulename_LTX_" (*modulename* is the name of the module). Internal symbols must be named in such a way that they won't conflict with other modules, for example, by prefixing them with "_modulename_". Although some platforms support having the same symbols defined more than once it is generally not portable and it makes it impossible to dlpreopen such modules.

libltdl will automatically cut the prefix off to get the real name of the symbol. Additionally, it supports modules that do not use a prefix so that you can also dlopen non-libtool modules.

`foo1.c` gives an example of a portable libtool module. Exported symbols are prefixed with "foo1_LTX_", internal symbols with "_foo1_". Aliases are defined at the beginning so that the code is more readable.

```
/* aliases for the exported symbols */
#define foo  foo1_LTX_foo
#define bar  foo1_LTX_bar

/* a global variable definition */
int bar = 1;

/* a private function */
int _foo1_helper() {
  return bar;
}

/* an exported function */
int foo() {
  return _foo1_helper();
}
```

The `Makefile.am` contains the necessary rules to build the module `foo1.la`:

```
...
lib_LTLIBRARIES = foo1.la

foo1_la_SOURCES = foo1.c
foo1_la_LDFLAGS = -module
```

...

11.3 Using libltdl in a multi threaded environment

Libltdl provides a wrapper around whatever dynamic run-time object loading mechanisms are provided by the host system, many of which are themselves not thread safe. Consequently libltdl cannot itself be consistently thread safe.

If you wish to use libltdl in a multithreaded environment, then you must mutex lock around libltdl calls, since they may in turn be calling non-thread-safe system calls on some target hosts.

Some old releases of libtool provided a mutex locking API that was unusable with POSIX threads, so callers were forced to lock around all libltdl API calls anyway. That mutex locking API was next to useless, and is not present in current releases.

Some future release of libtool may provide a new POSIX thread compliant mutex locking API.

11.4 Data associated with loaded modules

Some of the internal information about each loaded module that is maintained by libltdl is available to the user, in the form of this structure:

struct lt_dlinfo *{ char ***filename***; char ***name***; int ***ref_count***;*   [Type]
    *int ***is_resident***; int ***is_symglobal***; int ***is_symlocal***;}*
    lt_dlinfo is used to store information about a module. The *filename* attribute is a null-terminated character string of the real module file name. If the module is a libtool module then *name* is its module name (e.g. "libfoo" for "dir/libfoo.la"), otherwise it is set to NULL. The *ref_count* attribute is a reference counter that describes how often the same module is currently loaded. The remaining fields can be compared to any hints that were passed to lt_dlopenadvise to determine whether the underlying loader was able to follow them.

The following function will return a pointer to libltdl's internal copy of this structure for the given *handle*:

const lt_dlinfo * lt_dlgetinfo (*lt_dlhandle* **handle**)   [Function]
    Return a pointer to a struct that contains some information about the module *handle*. The contents of the struct must not be modified. Return NULL on failure.

Furthermore, to save you from having to keep a list of the handles of all the modules you have loaded, these functions allow you to iterate over libltdl's list of loaded modules:

lt_dlinterface_id   [Type]
    The opaque type used to hold the module interface details for each registered libltdl client.

int lt_dlhandle_interface (*lt_dlhandle* **handle**,   [Type]
    const char ***id_string***)
    Functions of this type are called to check that a handle conforms to a library's expected module interface when iterating over the global handle list. You should be

careful to write a callback function of this type that can correctly identify modules that belong to this client, both to prevent other clients from accidentally finding your loaded modules with the iterator functions below, and vice versa. The best way to do this is to check that module *handle* conforms to the interface specification of your loader using `lt_dlsym`.

The callback may be given **every** module loaded by all the libltdl module clients in the current address space, including any modules loaded by other libraries such as libltdl itself, and should return non-zero if that module does not fulfill the interface requirements of your loader.

```
int
my_interface_cb (lt_dlhandle handle, const char *id_string)
{
    char *(*module_id) (void) = NULL;

    /* A valid my_module must provide all of these symbols.  */
    if (!((module_id = (char*(*)(void)) lt_dlsym ("module_version"))
          && lt_dlsym ("my_module_entrypoint")))
        return 1;

    if (strcmp (id_string, module_id()) != 0)
        return 1;

    return 0;
}
```

`lt_dlinterface_id lt_dlinterface_register`   [Function]
        (*const char *id_string*, *lt_dlhandle_interface *iface*)
> Use this function to register your interface validator with libltdl, and in return obtain a unique key to store and retrieve per-module data. You supply an *id_string* and *iface* so that the resulting `lt_dlinterface_id` can be used to filter the module handles returned by the iteration functions below. If *iface* is `NULL`, all modules will be matched.

`void lt_dlinterface_free` (*lt_dlinterface_id *iface*)   [Function]
> Release the data associated with *iface*.

`int lt_dlhandle_map` (*lt_dlinterface_id *iface*,   [Function]
        int (*func) (lt_dlhandle *handle, *void * data*), *void * data*)
> For each module that matches *iface*, call the function *func*. When writing the *func* callback function, the argument *handle* is the handle of a loaded module, and *data* is the last argument passed to `lt_dlhandle_map`. As soon as *func* returns a non-zero value for one of the handles, `lt_dlhandle_map` will stop calling *func* and immediately return that non-zero value. Otherwise 0 is eventually returned when *func* has been successfully called for all matching modules.

lt_dlhandle lt_dlhandle_iterate (*lt_dlinterface_id* **iface**,   [Function]
        lt_dlhandle **place**)

> Iterate over the module handles loaded by *iface*, returning the first matching handle
> in the list if *place* is NULL, and the next one on subsequent calls. If *place* is the last
> element in the list of eligible modules, this function returns NULL.

```
lt_dlhandle handle = 0;
lt_dlinterface_id iface = my_interface_id;

while ((handle = lt_dlhandle_iterate (iface, handle)))
  {
    ...
  }
```

lt_dlhandle lt_dlhandle_fetch (*lt_dlinterface_id* **iface**,   [Function]
        const char ***module_name**)

> Search through the module handles loaded by *iface* for a module named *module_name*,
> returning its handle if found or else NULL if no such named module has been loaded
> by *iface*.

However, you might still need to maintain your own list of loaded module handles (in
parallel with the list maintained inside libltdl) if there were any other data that your
application wanted to associate with each open module. Instead, you can use the following
API calls to do that for you. You must first obtain a unique interface id from libltdl as
described above, and subsequently always use it to retrieve the data you stored earlier.
This allows different libraries to each store their own data against loaded modules, without
interfering with one another.

void * lt_dlcaller_set_data (*lt_dlinterface_id* **key**,   [Function]
        lt_dlhandle **handle**, *void* * **data**)

> Set *data* as the set of data uniquely associated with *key* and *handle* for later retrieval.
> This function returns the *data* previously associated with *key* and *handle* if any. A
> result of 0, may indicate that a diagnostic for the last error (if any) is available from
> lt_dlerror().
>
> For example, to correctly remove some associated data:

```
void *stale = lt_dlcaller_set_data (key, handle, 0);
if (stale != NULL)
  {
    free (stale);
  }
else
  {
    char *error_msg = lt_dlerror ();

    if (error_msg != NULL)
      {
        my_error_handler (error_msg);
        return STATUS_FAILED;
```

```
        }
    }
```

void * lt_dlcaller_get_data (*lt_dlinterface_id* **key**,   [Function]
    lt_dlhandle **handle**)

> Return the address of the data associated with *key* and *handle*, or else NULL if there is none.

Old versions of libltdl also provided a simpler, but similar, API based around **lt_dlcaller_id**. Unfortunately, it had no provision for detecting whether a module belonged to a particular interface as libltdl didn't support multiple loaders in the same address space at that time. Those APIs are no longer supported as there would be no way to stop clients of the old APIs from seeing (and accidentally altering) modules loaded by other libraries.

11.5 How to create and register new module loaders

Sometimes libltdl's many ways of gaining access to modules are not sufficient for the purposes of a project. You can write your own loader, and register it with libltdl so that **lt_dlopen** will be able to use it.

Writing a loader involves writing at least three functions that can be called by **lt_dlopen**, **lt_dlsym** and **lt_dlclose**. Optionally, you can provide a finalisation function to perform any cleanup operations when **lt_dlexit** executes, and a symbol prefix string that will be prepended to any symbols passed to **lt_dlsym**. These functions must match the function pointer types below, after which they can be allocated to an instance of **lt_user_dlloader** and registered.

Registering the loader requires that you choose a name for it, so that it can be recognised by **lt_dlloader_find** and removed with **lt_dlloader_remove**. The name you choose must be unique, and not already in use by libltdl's builtin loaders:

"dlopen"   The system dynamic library loader, if one exists.

"dld"   The GNU dld loader, if **libdld** was installed when libltdl was built.

"dlpreload"
            The loader for **lt_dlopen**ing of preloaded static modules.

The prefix "dl" is reserved for loaders supplied with future versions of libltdl, so you should not use that for your own loader names.

The following types are defined in **ltdl.h**:

lt_module   [Type]

> **lt_module** is a dlloader dependent module. The dynamic module loader extensions communicate using these low level types.

lt_dlloader   [Type]

> **lt_dlloader** is a handle for module loader types.

lt_user_data   [Type]

> **lt_user_data** is used for specifying loader instance data.

struct **lt_user_dlloader** *{const char *`sym_prefix`;*   [Type]
       lt_module_open *`module_open`; lt_module_close *`module_close`;
       lt_find_sym *`find_sym`; lt_dlloader_exit *`dlloader_exit`; }
     If you want to define a new way to open dynamic modules, and have the `lt_dlopen`
 API use it, you need to instantiate one of these structures and pass it to `lt_dlloader_`
 `add`. You can pass whatever you like in the *dlloader_data* field, and it will be passed
 back as the value of the first parameter to each of the functions specified in the
 function pointer fields.

lt_module **lt_module_open** (*const char *`filename`*)   [Type]
     The type of the loader function for an `lt_dlloader` module loader. The value set in
 the dlloader_data field of the **struct lt_user_dlloader** structure will be passed into
 this function in the *loader_data* parameter. Implementation of such a function should
 attempt to load the named module, and return an `lt_module` suitable for passing
 in to the associated `lt_module_close` and `lt_sym_find` function pointers. If the
 function fails it should return NULL, and set the error message with `lt_dlseterror`.

int **lt_module_close** (*lt_user_data* `loader_data`, *lt_module* `module`)   [Type]
     The type of the unloader function for a user defined module loader. Implementation
 of such a function should attempt to release any resources tied up by the *module*
 module, and then unload it from memory. If the function fails for some reason, set
 the error message with `lt_dlseterror` and return non-zero.

void * **lt_find_sym** (*lt_module* `module`, *const char *`symbol`*)   [Type]
     The type of the symbol lookup function for a user defined module loader. Imple-
 mentation of such a function should return the address of the named *symbol* in the
 module *module*, or else set the error message with `lt_dlseterror` and return NULL
 if lookup fails.

int **lt_dlloader_exit** (*lt_user_data* `loader_data`)   [Type]
     The type of the finalisation function for a user defined module loader. Implementation
 of such a function should free any resources associated with the loader, including any
 user specified data in the **dlloader_data** field of the **lt_user_dlloader**. If non-NULL,
 the function will be called by `lt_dlexit`, and `lt_dlloader_remove`.

For example:

```
int
register_myloader (void)
{
  lt_user_dlloader dlloader;

  /* User modules are responsible for their own initialisation. */
  if (myloader_init () != 0)
    return MYLOADER_INIT_ERROR;

  dlloader.sym_prefix   = NULL;
  dlloader.module_open  = myloader_open;
  dlloader.module_close = myloader_close;
```

```
    dlloader.find_sym     = myloader_find_sym;
    dlloader.dlloader_exit = myloader_exit;
    dlloader.dlloader_data = (lt_user_data)myloader_function;

    /* Add my loader as the default module loader. */
    if (lt_dlloader_add (lt_dlloader_next (NULL), &dlloader,
                         "myloader") != 0)
      return ERROR;

    return OK;
  }
```

Note that if there is any initialisation required for the loader, it must be performed manually before the loader is registered – libltdl doesn't handle user loader initialisation.

Finalisation *is* handled by libltdl however, and it is important to ensure the **dlloader_exit** callback releases any resources claimed during the initialisation phase.

libltdl provides the following functions for writing your own module loaders:

int lt_dlloader_add (*lt_dlloader *place*, *lt_user_dlloader *dlloader*,   [Function]
      const char *loader_name)
> Add a new module loader to the list of all loaders, either as the last loader (if *place* is NULL), else immediately before the loader passed as *place*. *loader_name* will be returned by lt_dlloader_name if it is subsequently passed a newly registered loader. These *loader_names* must be unique, or lt_dlloader_remove and lt_dlloader_find cannot work. Returns 0 for success.
>
> ```
> /* Make myloader be the last one. */
> if (lt_dlloader_add (NULL, myloader) != 0)
>   perror (lt_dlerror ());
> ```

int lt_dlloader_remove (*const char *loader_name*)   [Function]
> Remove the loader identified by the unique name, *loader_name*. Before this can succeed, all modules opened by the named loader must have been closed. Returns 0 for success, otherwise an error message can be obtained from lt_dlerror.
>
> ```
> /* Remove myloader. */
> if (lt_dlloader_remove ("myloader") != 0)
>   perror (lt_dlerror ());
> ```

lt_dlloader * lt_dlloader_next (*lt_dlloader *place*)   [Function]
> Iterate over the module loaders, returning the first loader if *place* is NULL, and the next one on subsequent calls. The handle is for use with lt_dlloader_add.
>
> ```
> /* Make myloader be the first one. */
> if (lt_dlloader_add (lt_dlloader_next (NULL), myloader) != 0)
>   return ERROR;
> ```

lt_dlloader * lt_dlloader_find (*const char *loader_name*)   [Function]
> Return the first loader with a matching *loader_name* identifier, or else NULL, if the identifier is not found.
>
> The identifiers that may be used by libltdl itself, if the host architecture supports them are *dlopen*[1], *dld* and *dlpreload*.
>
> ```
> /* Add a user loader as the next module loader to be tried if
>    the standard dlopen loader were to fail when lt_dlopening. */
> if (lt_dlloader_add (lt_dlloader_find ("dlopen"), myloader) != 0)
>   return ERROR;
> ```

const char * lt_dlloader_name (*lt_dlloader *place*)   [Function]
> Return the identifying name of *place*, as obtained from lt_dlloader_next or lt_dlloader_find. If this function fails, it will return NULL and set an error for retrieval with lt_dlerror.

lt_user_data * lt_dlloader_data (*lt_dlloader *place*)   [Function]
> Return the address of the dlloader_data of *place*, as obtained from lt_dlloader_next or lt_dlloader_find. If this function fails, it will return NULL and set an error for retrieval with lt_dlerror.

---

[1] This is used for the host dependent module loading API – shl_load and LoadLibrary for example

11.5.1 Error handling within user module loaders

int lt_dladderror (*const char *diagnostic*)   [Function]

>   This function allows you to integrate your own error messages into lt_dlerror. Pass
>   in a suitable diagnostic message for return by lt_dlerror, and an error identifier for
>   use with lt_dlseterror is returned.
>
>   If the allocation of an identifier fails, this function returns -1.

```
        int myerror = lt_dladderror ("doh!");
        if (myerror < 0)
          perror (lt_dlerror ());
```

int lt_dlseterror (*int errorcode*)   [Function]

>   When writing your own module loaders, you should use this function to raise errors
>   so that they are propagated through the lt_dlerror interface. All of the standard
>   errors used by libltdl are declared in ltdl.h, or you can add more of your own with
>   lt_dladderror. This function returns 0 on success.

```
        if (lt_dlseterror (LTDL_ERROR_NO_MEMORY) != 0)
          porror (lt_dlerror ());
```

11.6 How to distribute libltdl with your package

Even though libltdl is installed together with libtool, you may wish to include libltdl in the
distribution of your package, for the convenience of users of your package that don't have
libtool or libltdl installed, or if you are using features of a very new version of libltdl that
you don't expect your users to have yet. In such cases, you must decide what flavor of
libltdl you want to use: a convenience library or an installable libtool library.

   The most simplistic way to add libltdl to your package is to copy all the libltdl
source files to a subdirectory within your package and to build and link them along with
the rest of your sources. To help you do this, the m4 macros for Autoconf are available in
ltdl.m4. You must ensure that they are available in aclocal.m4 before you run Autoconf[2].
Having made the macros available, you must add a call to the 'LTDL_INIT' macro (after
the call to 'LT_INIT') to your package's configure.ac to perform the configure time checks
required to build the library correctly. Unfortunately, this method has problems if you
then try to link the package binaries with an installed libltdl, or a library that depends on
libltdl, because of the duplicate symbol definitions. For example, ultimately linking against
two different versions of libltdl, or against both a local convenience library and an installed
libltdl is bad. Ensuring that only one copy of the libltdl sources are linked into any program
is left as an exercise for the reader.

LT_CONFIG_LTDL_DIR (*directory*)   [Macro]

>   Declare *directory* to be the location of the libltdl source files, for libtoolize
>   --ltdl to place them. See Section 5.5.1 [Invoking libtoolize], page 35, for more
>   details. Provided that you add an appropriate LT_CONFIG_LTDL_DIR call in your
>   configure.ac before calling libtoolize, the appropriate libltdl files will be in-
>   stalled automatically.

---

[2] We used to recommend adding the contents of ltdl.m4 to acinclude.m4, but with aclocal from a
    modern Automake (1.8 or newer) and this release of libltdl that is not only unnecessary but makes it
    easy to forget to upgrade acinclude.m4 if you move to a different release of libltdl.

LTDL_INIT (*options*)   [Macro]
LT_WITH_LTDL   [Macro]
AC_WITH_LTDL   [Macro]
>   AC_WITH_LTDL and LT_WITH_LTDL are deprecated names for older versions of this
>   macro; autoupdate will update your configure.ac file.
>
>   This macro adds the following options to the configure script:
>
>   --with-ltdl-include *installed-ltdl-header-dir*
>>   The LTDL_INIT macro will look in the standard header file locations to
>>   find the installed libltdl headers. If LTDL_INIT can't find them by itself,
>>   the person who builds your package can use this option to tell configure
>>   where the installed libltdl headers are.
>
>   --with-ltdl-lib *installed-ltdl-library-dir*
>>   Similarly, the person building your package can use this option to help
>>   configure find the installed libltdl.la.
>
>   --with-included-ltdl
>>   If there is no installed libltdl, or in any case if the person building your
>>   package would rather use the libltdl sources shipped with the package
>>   in the subdirectory named by LT_CONFIG_LTDL_DIR, they should pass
>>   this option to configure.
>
>   If the --with-included-ltdl is not passed at configure time, and an installed
>   libltdl is not found[3], then configure will exit immediately with an error that
>   asks the user to either specify the location of an installed libltdl using the
>   --with-ltdl-include and --with-ltdl-lib options, or to build with the libltdl
>   sources shipped with the package by passing --with-included-ltdl.
>
>   If an installed libltdl is found, then LIBLTDL is set to the link flags needed to use
>   it, and LTDLINCL to the preprocessor flags needed to find the installed headers, and
>   LTDLDEPS will be empty. Note, however, that no version checking is performed. You
>   should manually check for the libltdl features you need in configure.ac:
>
>```
>        LT_INIT([dlopen])
>        LTDL_INIT
>
>        # The lt_dladvise_init symbol was added with libtool-2.2
>        if test yes != "$with_included_ltdl"; then
>          save_CFLAGS=$CFLAGS
>          save_LDFLAGS=$LDFLAGS
>          CFLAGS="$CFLAGS $LTDLINCL"
>          LDFLAGS="$LDFLAGS $LIBLTDL"
>          AC_CHECK_LIB([ltdl], [lt_dladvise_init],
>                       [],
>              [AC_MSG_ERROR([installed libltdl is too old])])
>          LDFLAGS=$save_LDFLAGS
>          CFLAGS=$save_CFLAGS
>```

---

[3] Even if libltdl is installed, 'LTDL_INIT' may fail to detect it if libltdl depends on symbols provided by libraries other than the C library.

```
    fi
```

options may include no more than one of the following build modes depending on how you want your project to build `libltdl`: 'nonrecursive', 'recursive', or 'subproject'. In order for `libtoolize` to detect this option correctly, if you supply one of these arguments, they must be given literally (i.e., macros or shell variables that expand to the correct ltdl mode will not work).

'nonrecursive'

> This is how the Libtool project distribution builds the `libltdl` we ship and install. If you wish to use Automake to build `libltdl` without invoking a recursive make to descend into the `libltdl` subdirectory, then use this option. You will need to set your configuration up carefully to make this work properly, and you will need releases of Autoconf and Automake that support `subdir-objects` and `LIBOBJDIR` properly. In your `configure.ac`, add:

```
AM_INIT_AUTOMAKE([subdir-objects])
AC_CONFIG_HEADERS([config.h])
LT_CONFIG_LTDL_DIR([libltdl])
LT_INIT([dlopen])
LTDL_INIT([nonrecursive])
```

> You *have to* use a config header, but it may have a name different than `config.h`.

> Also, add the following near the top of your `Makefile.am`:

```
AM_CPPFLAGS =
AM_LDFLAGS =

BUILT_SOURCES =
EXTRA_DIST =
CLEANFILES =
MOSTLYCLEANFILES =

include_HEADERS =
noinst_LTLIBRARIES =
lib_LTLIBRARIES =
EXTRA_LTLIBRARIES =

include libltdl/ltdl.mk
```

> Unless you build no other libraries from this `Makefile.am`, you will also need to change `lib_LTLIBRARIES` to assign with '+=' so that the `libltdl` targets declared in `ltdl.mk` are not overwritten.

'recursive'

> This build mode still requires that you use Automake, but (in contrast with 'nonrecursive') uses the more usual device of starting another **make** process in the `libltdl` subdirectory. To use this mode, you should add to your `configure.ac`:

```
AM_INIT_AUTOMAKE
AC_CONFIG_HEADERS([config.h])
LT_CONFIG_LTDL_DIR([libltdl])
LT_INIT([dlopen])
LTDL_INIT([recursive])
AC_CONFIG_FILES([libltdl/Makefile])
```

Again, you *have to* use a config header, but it may have a name different than config.h if you like.

Also, add this to your Makefile.am:

```
SUBDIRS = libltdl
```

'subproject'

This mode is the default unless you explicitly add **recursive** or **nonrecursive** to your LTDL_INIT options; subproject is the only mode supported by previous releases of libltdl. Even if you do not use Autoconf in the parent project, then, in 'subproject' mode, still libltdl contains all the necessary files to configure and build itself – you just need to arrange for your build system to call libltdl/configure with appropriate options, and then run make in the libltdl subdirectory.

If you *are* using Autoconf and Automake, then you will need to add the following to your configure.ac:

```
LT_CONFIG_LTDL_DIR([libltdl])
LTDL_INIT
```

and to Makefile.am:

```
SUBDIRS = libltdl
```

Aside from setting the libltdl build mode, there are other keywords that you can pass to LTDL_INIT to modify its behavior when --with-included-ltdl has been given:

'convenience'

This is the default unless you explicitly add **installable** to your LTDL_ INIT options.

This keyword will cause options to be passed to the configure script in the subdirectory named by LT_CONFIG_LTDL_DIR to cause it to be built as a convenience library. If you're not using automake, you will need to define top_build_prefix, top_builddir, and top_srcdir in your makefile so that LIBLTDL, LTDLDEPS, and LTDLINCL expand correctly.

One advantage of the convenience library is that it is not installed, so the fact that you use libltdl will not be apparent to the user, and it won't overwrite a pre-installed version of libltdl the system might already have in the installation directory. On the other hand, if you want to upgrade libltdl for any reason (e.g. a bugfix) you'll have to recompile your package instead of just replacing the shared installed version of libltdl. However, if your programs or libraries are linked with other libraries that use such a pre-installed version of libltdl, you may get linker errors or run-time crashes. Another problem is that you cannot link the convenience library into more than one libtool library, then link a single program with those libraries, because you may get duplicate symbols. In general you can safely use the convenience library in programs that don't depend on other libraries that might use `libltdl` too.

'installable'

> This keyword will pass options to the `configure` script in the subdirectory named by `LT_CONFIG_LTDL_DIR` to cause it to be built as an installable library. If you're not using automake, you will need to define `top_build_prefix`, `top_builddir` and `top_srcdir` in your makefile so that `LIBLTDL`, `LTDLDEPS`, and `LTDLINCL` are expanded properly.
>
> Be aware that you could overwrite another `libltdl` already installed to the same directory if you use this option.

Whatever method you use, 'LTDL_INIT' will define the shell variable `LIBLTDL` to the link flag that you should use to link with `libltdl`, the shell variable `LTDLDEPS` to the files that can be used as a dependency in `Makefile` rules, and the shell variable `LTDLINCL` to the preprocessor flag that you should use to compile programs that include `ltdl.h`. So, when you want to link a program with libltdl, be it a convenience, installed or installable library, just use '$(LTDLINCL)' for preprocessing and compilation, and '$(LIBLTDL)' for linking.

- If your package is built using an installed version of `libltdl`, `LIBLTDL` will be set to the compiler flags needed to link against the installed library, `LTDLDEPS` will be empty, and `LTDLINCL` will be set to the compiler flags needed to find the `libltdl` header files.

- If your package is built using the convenience libltdl, `LIBLTDL` and `LTDLDEPS` will be the pathname for the convenience version of libltdl (starting with '${top_builddir}/' or '${top_build_prefix}') and `LTDLINCL` will be -I followed by the directory that contains `ltdl.h` (starting with '${top_srcdir}/').

- If an installable version of the included `libltdl` is being built, its pathname starting with '${top_builddir}/' or '${top_build_prefix}', will be stored in `LIBLTDL` and `LTDLDEPS`, and `LTDLINCL` will be set just like in the case of convenience library.

You should probably also use the 'dlopen' option to `LT_INIT` in your `configure.ac`, otherwise libtool will assume no dlopening mechanism is supported, and revert to dlpreopening, which is probably not what you want. Avoid using the `-static`, `-static-libtool-libs`, or `-all-static` switches when linking programs with libltdl. This will not work on all platforms, because the dlopening functions may not be available for static linking.

The following example shows you how to embed an installable libltdl in your package. In order to use the convenience variant, just replace the `LTDL_INIT` option 'installable' with 'convenience'. We assume that libltdl was embedded using 'libtoolize --ltdl'.

configure.ac:

```
...
# Name the subdirectory that contains libltdl sources
LT_CONFIG_LTDL_DIR([libltdl])

# Configure libtool with dlopen support if possible
LT_INIT([dlopen])

# Enable building of the installable libltdl library
```

```
    LTDL_INIT([installable])
    ...
Makefile.am:

    ...
    SUBDIRS = libltdl

    AM_CPPFLAGS = $(LTDLINCL)

    myprog_LDFLAGS = -export-dynamic
    myprog_LDADD = $(LIBLTDL) -dlopen self -dlopen foo1.la
    myprog_DEPENDENCIES = $(LTDLDEPS) foo1.la
    ...
```

LTDL_INSTALLABLE   [Macro]
AC_LIBLTDL_INSTALLABLE   [Macro]

> These macros are deprecated, the 'installable' option to LTDL_INIT should be used
> instead.

LTDL_CONVENIENCE   [Macro]
AC_LIBLTDL_CONVENIENCE   [Macro]

> These macros are deprecated, the 'convenience' option to LTDL_INIT should be used
> instead.

12 Libtool's trace interface

This section describes macros whose sole purpose is to be traced using Autoconf's `--trace` option (see Section "The Autoconf Manual" in *The Autoconf Manual*) to query the Libtool configuration of a project. These macros are called by Libtool internals and should never be called by user code; they should only be traced.

LT_SUPPORTED_TAG (tag)   [Macro]

This macro is called once for each language enabled in the package. Its only argument, *tag*, is the tag-name corresponding to the language (see Section 6.2 [Tags], page 39).

You can therefore retrieve the list of all tags enabled in a project using the following command:

```
autoconf --trace 'LT_SUPPORTED_TAG:$1'
```

13 Frequently Asked Questions about libtool

This chapter covers some questions that often come up on the mailing lists.

13.1 Why does libtool strip link flags when creating a library?

When creating a shared library, but not when compiling or creating a program, `libtool` drops some flags from the command line provided by the user. This is done because flags unknown to `libtool` may interfere with library creation or require additional support from `libtool`, and because omitting flags is usually the conservative choice for a successful build.

If you encounter flags that you think are useful to pass, as a work-around you can prepend flags with `-Wc,` or `-Xcompiler` to allow them to be passed through to the compiler driver (see Section 4.2 [Link mode], page 18). Another possibility is to add flags already to the compiler command at `configure` run time:

```
./configure CC='gcc -m64'
```

If you think `libtool` should let some flag through by default, here's how you can test such an inclusion: grab the Libtool development tree, edit the `ltmain.in` file in the `libltdl/config` subdirectory to pass through the flag (search for 'Flags to be passed through'), re-bootstrap and build with the flags in question added to `LDFLAGS`, `CFLAGS`, `CXXFLAGS`, etc. on the `configure` command line as appropriate. Run the testsuite as described in the `README` file and report results to the Libtool bug reporting address `bug-libtool@gnu.org`.

14 Troubleshooting

Libtool is under constant development, changing to remain up-to-date with modern operating systems. If libtool doesn't work the way you think it should on your platform, you should read this chapter to help determine what the problem is, and how to resolve it.

14.1 The libtool test suite

Libtool comes with two integrated sets of tests to check that your build is sane, that test its capabilities, and report obvious bugs in the libtool program. These tests, too, are constantly evolving, based on past problems with libtool, and known deficiencies in other operating systems.

As described in the `README` file, you may run *make -k check* after you have built libtool (possibly before you install it) to make sure that it meets basic functional requirements.

14.1.1 Description of test suite

Here is a list of the current programs in the old test suite, and what they test for:

```
cdemo-conf.test
cdemo-make.test
cdemo-exec.test
cdemo-static.test
cdemo-static-make.test
cdemo-static-exec.test
cdemo-shared.test
cdemo-shared-make.test
cdemo-shared-exec.test
cdemo-undef.test
cdemo-undef-make.test
cdemo-undef-exec.test
```

> These programs check to see that the `tests/cdemo` subdirectory of the libtool distribution can be configured and built correctly.
>
> The `tests/cdemo` subdirectory contains a demonstration of libtool convenience libraries, a mechanism that allows build-time static libraries to be created, in a way that their components can be later linked into programs or other libraries, even shared ones.
>
> The tests matching `cdemo-*make.test` and `cdemo-*exec.test` are executed three times, under three different libtool configurations: `cdemo-conf.test` configures `cdemo/libtool` to build both static and shared libraries (the default for platforms that support both), `cdemo-static.test` builds only static libraries ('--disable-shared'), and `cdemo-shared.test` builds only shared libraries ('--disable-static').
>
> The test `cdemo-undef.test` tests the generation of shared libraries with undefined symbols on systems that allow this.

```
demo-conf.test
demo-make.test
demo-exec.test
demo-inst.test
demo-unst.test
demo-static.test
demo-static-make.test
demo-static-exec.test
demo-static-inst.test
demo-static-unst.test
demo-shared.test
demo-shared-make.test
demo-shared-exec.test
demo-shared-inst.test
demo-shared-unst.test
demo-nofast.test
demo-nofast-make.test
demo-nofast-exec.test
demo-nofast-inst.test
demo-nofast-unst.test
demo-pic.test
demo-pic-make.test
demo-pic-exec.test
demo-nopic.test
demo-nopic-make.test
demo-nopic-exec.test
```

These programs check to see that the `tests/demo` subdirectory of the libtool distribution can be configured, built, installed, and uninstalled correctly.

The `tests/demo` subdirectory contains a demonstration of a trivial package that uses libtool. The tests matching `demo-*make.test`, `demo-*exec.test`, `demo-*inst.test` and `demo-*unst.test` are executed four times, under four different libtool configurations: `demo-conf.test` configures `demo/libtool` to build both static and shared libraries, `demo-static.test` builds only static libraries (`--disable-shared`), and `demo-shared.test` builds only shared libraries (`--disable-static`). `demo-nofast.test` configures `demo/libtool` to disable the fast-install mode (`--enable-fast-install=no`). `demo-pic.test` configures `demo/libtool` to prefer building PIC code (`--with-pic`), `demo-nopic.test` to prefer non-PIC code (`--without-pic`).

`demo-deplibs.test`

Many systems cannot link static libraries into shared libraries. libtool uses a `deplibs_check_method` to prevent such cases. This tests checks whether libtool's `deplibs_check_method` works properly.

`demo-hardcode.test`

On all systems with shared libraries, the location of the library can be encoded in executables that are linked against it see Section 3.3 [Linking executables], page 7. This test checks under what conditions your system linker hardcodes the library location, and guarantees that they correspond to libtool's own notion of how your linker behaves.

`demo-relink.test`
`depdemo-relink.test`

These tests check whether variable `shlibpath_overrides_runpath` is properly set. If the test fails, it will indicate what the variable should have been set to.

`demo-noinst-link.test`

Checks whether libtool will not try to link with a previously installed version of a library when it should be linking with a just-built one.

`depdemo-conf.test`
`depdemo-make.test`
`depdemo-exec.test`
`depdemo-inst.test`
`depdemo-unst.test`
`depdemo-static.test`
`depdemo-static-make.test`
`depdemo-static-exec.test`
`depdemo-static-inst.test`
`depdemo-static-unst.test`
`depdemo-shared.test`
`depdemo-shared-make.test`
`depdemo-shared-exec.test`
`depdemo-shared-inst.test`
`depdemo-shared-unst.test`
`depdemo-nofast.test`
`depdemo-nofast-make.test`
`depdemo-nofast-exec.test`
`depdemo-nofast-inst.test`
`depdemo-nofast-unst.test`

These programs check to see that the `tests/depdemo` subdirectory of the libtool distribution can be configured, built, installed, and uninstalled correctly.

The `tests/depdemo` subdirectory contains a demonstration of inter-library dependencies with libtool. The test programs link some interdependent libraries.

The tests matching `depdemo-*make.test`, `depdemo-*exec.test`, `depdemo-*inst.test` and `depdemo-*unst.test` are executed four times, under four different libtool configurations: `depdemo-conf.test` configures `depdemo/libtool` to build both static and shared libraries, `depdemo-static.test` builds only static libraries (`--disable-shared`), and `depdemo-shared.test` builds only shared libraries (`--disable-static`). `depdemo-nofast.test` configures `depdemo/libtool` to disable the fast-install mode (`--enable-fast-install=no`).

```
mdemo-conf.test
mdemo-make.test
mdemo-exec.test
mdemo-inst.test
mdemo-unst.test
mdemo-static.test
mdemo-static-make.test
mdemo-static-exec.test
mdemo-static-inst.test
mdemo-static-unst.test
mdemo-shared.test
mdemo-shared-make.test
mdemo-shared-exec.test
mdemo-shared-inst.test
mdemo-shared-unst.test
```

These programs check to see that the `tests/mdemo` subdirectory of the libtool distribution can be configured, built, installed, and uninstalled correctly.

The `tests/mdemo` subdirectory contains a demonstration of a package that uses libtool and the system independent dlopen wrapper `libltdl` to load modules. The library `libltdl` provides a dlopen wrapper for various platforms (POSIX) including support for dlpreopened modules (see Section 10.2 [Dlpreopening], page 49).

The tests matching `mdemo-*make.test`, `mdemo-*exec.test`, `mdemo-*inst.test` and `mdemo-*unst.test` are executed three times, under three different libtool configurations: `mdemo-conf.test` configures `mdemo/libtool` to build both static and shared libraries, `mdemo-static.test` builds only static libraries (`--disable-shared`), and `mdemo-shared.test` builds only shared libraries (`--disable-static`).

```
mdemo-dryrun.test
```

This test checks whether libtool's `--dry-run` mode works properly.

```
mdemo2-conf.test
mdemo2-exec.test
mdemo2-make.test
```

These programs check to see that the `tests/mdemo2` subdirectory of the libtool distribution can be configured, built, and executed correctly.

The `tests/mdemo2` directory contains a demonstration of a package that attempts to link with a library (from the `tests/mdemo` directory) that itself does dlopening of libtool modules.

```
link.test
```

This test guarantees that linking directly against a non-libtool static library works properly.

```
link-2.test
```

This test makes sure that files ending in `.lo` are never linked directly into a program file.

`nomode.test`

> Check whether we can actually get help for libtool.

`objectlist.test`

> Check that a nonexistent objectlist file is properly detected.

`pdemo-conf.test`
`pdemo-make.test`
`pdemo-exec.test`
`pdemo-inst.test`

> These programs check to see that the `tests/pdemo` subdirectory of the libtool distribution can be configured, built, and executed correctly.
>
> The `pdemo-conf.test` lowers the `max_cmd_len` variable in the generated libtool script to test the measures to evade command line length limitations.

`quote.test`

> This program checks libtool's metacharacter quoting.

`sh.test`   Checks for some nonportable or dubious or undesired shell constructs in shell scripts.

`suffix.test`

> When other programming languages are used with libtool (see Chapter 6 [Other languages], page 39), the source files may end in suffixes other than `.c`. This test validates that libtool can handle suffixes for all the file types that it supports, and that it fails when the suffix is invalid.

`tagdemo-conf.test`
`tagdemo-make.test`
`tagdemo-exec.test`
`tagdemo-static.test`
`tagdemo-static-make.test`
`tagdemo-static-exec.test`
`tagdemo-shared.test`
`tagdemo-shared-make.test`
`tagdemo-shared-exec.test`
`tagdemo-undef.test`
`tagdemo-undef-make.test`
`tagdemo-undef-exec.test`

> These programs check to see that the `tests/tagdemo` subdirectory of the libtool distribution can be configured, built, and executed correctly.
>
> The `tests/tagdemo` directory contains a demonstration of a package that uses libtool's multi-language support through configuration tags. It generates a library from C++ sources, which is then linked to a C++ program.

```
f77demo-conf.test
f77demo-make.test
f77demo-exec.test
f77demo-static.test
f77demo-static-make.test
f77demo-static-exec.test
f77demo-shared.test
f77demo-shared-make.test
f77demo-shared-exec.test
```

These programs check to see that the `tests/f77demo` subdirectory of the libtool distribution can be configured, built, and executed correctly.

The `tests/f77demo` tests test Fortran 77 support in libtool by creating libraries from Fortran 77 sources, and mixed Fortran and C sources, and a Fortran 77 program to use the former library, and a C program to use the latter library.

```
fcdemo-conf.test
fcdemo-make.test
fcdemo-exec.test
fcdemo-static.test
fcdemo-static-make.test
fcdemo-static-exec.test
fcdemo-shared.test
fcdemo-shared-make.test
fcdemo-shared-exec.test
```

These programs check to see that the `tests/fcdemo` subdirectory of the libtool distribution can be configured, built, and executed correctly.

The `tests/fcdemo` is similar to the `tests/f77demo` directory, except that Fortran 90 is used in combination with the 'FC' interface provided by Autoconf and Automake.

The new, Autotest-based test suite uses keywords to classify certain test groups:

'CXX'
'F77'
'FC'
'GCJ'   The test group exercises one of these `libtool` language tags.

'autoconf'
'automake'
These keywords denote that the respective external program is needed by the test group. The tests are typically skipped if the program is not installed. The 'automake' keyword may also denote use of the `aclocal` program.

'interactive'
This test group may require user interaction on some systems. Typically, this means closing a popup window about a DLL load error on Windows.

'libltdl'   Denote that the `libltdl` library is exercised by the test group.

'libtool'
'libtoolize'
> Denote that the `libtool` or `libtoolize` scripts are exercised by the test group, respectively.

'recursive'
> Denote that this test group may recursively re-invoke the test suite itself, with changed settings and maybe a changed `libtool` script. You may use the `INNER_TESTSUITEFLAGS` variable to pass additional settings to this recursive invocation. Typically, recursive invocations delimit the set of tests with another keyword, for example by passing `-k libtool` right before the expansion of the `INNER_TESTSUITEFLAGS` variable (without an intervening space, so you get the chance for further delimitation).

> Test groups with the keyword 'recursive' should not be denoted with keywords, in order to avoid infinite recursion. As a consequence, recursive test groups themselves should never require user interaction, while the test groups they invoke may do so.

There is a convenience target 'check-noninteractive' that runs all tests from both test suites that do not cause user interaction on Windows. Conversely, the target 'check-interactive' runs the complement of tests and might require closing popup windows about DLL load errors on Windows.

14.1.2 When tests fail

When the tests in the old test suite are run via **make check**, output is caught in per-test `tests/test-name.log` files and summarized in the **test-suite.log** file. The exit status of each program tells the **Makefile** whether or not the test succeeded.

If a test fails, it means that there is either a programming error in libtool, or in the test program itself.

To investigate a particular test, you may run it directly, as you would a normal program. When the test is invoked in this way, it produces output that may be useful in determining what the problem is.

The new, Autotest-based test suite produces as output a file **tests/testsuite.log** that contains information about failed tests.

You can pass options to the test suite through the **make** variable TESTSUITEFLAGS (see Section "The Autoconf Manual" in *The Autoconf Manual*).

14.2 Reporting bugs

If you think you have discovered a bug in libtool, you should think twice: the libtool maintainer is notorious for passing the buck (or maybe that should be "passing the bug"). Libtool was invented to fix known deficiencies in shared library implementations, so, in a way, most of the bugs in libtool are actually bugs in other operating systems. However, the libtool maintainer would definitely be happy to add support for somebody else's buggy operating system. [I wish there was a good way to do winking smiley-faces in Texinfo.]

Genuine bugs in libtool include problems with shell script portability, documentation errors, and failures in the test suite (see Section 14.1 [Libtool test suite], page 76).

First, check the documentation and help screens to make sure that the behaviour you think is a problem is not already mentioned as a feature.

Then, you should read the Emacs guide to reporting bugs (see Section "Reporting Bugs" in *The Emacs Manual*). Some of the details listed there are specific to Emacs, but the principle behind them is a general one.

Finally, send a bug report to the Libtool bug reporting address `bug-libtool@gnu.org` with any appropriate *facts*, such as test suite output (see Section 14.1.2 [When tests fail], page 82), all the details needed to reproduce the bug, and a brief description of why you think the behaviour is a bug. Be sure to include the word "libtool" in the subject line, as well as the version number you are using (which can be found by typing `libtool --version`).

15 Maintenance notes for libtool

This chapter contains information that the libtool maintainer finds important. It will be of no use to you unless you are considering porting libtool to new systems, or writing your own libtool.

15.1 Porting libtool to new systems

Before you embark on porting libtool to an unsupported system, it is worthwhile to send e-mail to the Libtool mailing list `libtool@gnu.org`, to make sure that you are not duplicating existing work.

If you find that any porting documentation is missing, please complain! Complaints with patches and improvements to the documentation, or to libtool itself, are more than welcome.

15.1.1 Information sources

Once it is clear that a new port is necessary, you'll generally need the following information:

canonical system name
> You need the output of `config.guess` for this system, so that you can make changes to the libtool configuration process without affecting other systems.

man pages for `ld` and `cc`
> These generally describe what flags are used to generate PIC, to create shared libraries, and to link against only static libraries. You may need to follow some cross references to find the information that is required.

man pages for `ld.so`, `rtld`, or equivalent
> These are a valuable resource for understanding how shared libraries are loaded on the system.

man page for `ldconfig`, or equivalent
> This page usually describes how to install shared libraries.

output from `ls -l /lib /usr/lib`
> This shows the naming convention for shared libraries on the system, including what names should be symbolic links.

any additional documentation
> Some systems have special documentation on how to build and install shared libraries.

If you know how to program the Bourne shell, then you can complete the port yourself; otherwise, you'll have to find somebody with the relevant skills who will do the work. People on the libtool mailing list are usually willing to volunteer to help you with new ports, so you can send the information to them.

To do the port yourself, you'll definitely need to modify the `libtool.m4` macros to make platform-specific changes to the configuration process. You should search that file for the `PORTME` keyword, which will give you some hints on what you'll need to change. In general, all that is involved is modifying the appropriate configuration variables (see Section 15.4 [libtool script contents], page 100).

Your best bet is to find an already-supported system that is similar to yours, and make your changes based on that. In some cases, however, your system will differ significantly from every other supported system, and it may be necessary to add new configuration variables, and modify the `ltmain.in` script accordingly. Be sure to write to the mailing list before you make changes to `ltmain.in`, since they may have advice on the most effective way of accomplishing what you want.

15.1.2 Porting inter-library dependencies support

Since version 1.2c, libtool has re-introduced the ability to do inter-library dependency on some platforms, thanks to a patch by Toshio Kuratomi `badger@prtr-13.ucsc.edu`. Here's a shortened version of the message that contained his patch:

The basic architecture is this: in `libtool.m4`, the person who writes libtool makes sure '`$deplibs`' is included in '`$archive_cmds`' somewhere and also sets the variable '`$deplibs_check_method`', and maybe '`$file_magic_cmd`' when '`deplibs_check_method`' is file_magic.

'`deplibs_check_method`' can be one of five things:

'`file_magic [regex]`'

> looks in the library link path for libraries that have the right libname. Then it runs '`$file_magic_cmd`' on the library and checks for a match against the extended regular expression *regex*. When `file_magic_test_file` is set by `libtool.m4`, it is used as an argument to '`$file_magic_cmd`' to verify whether the regular expression matches its output, and warn the user otherwise.

'`test_compile`'

> just checks whether it is possible to link a program out of a list of libraries, and checks which of those are listed in the output of `ldd`. It is currently unused, and will probably be dropped in the future.

'`pass_all`'

> will pass everything without any checking. This may work on platforms where code is position-independent by default and inter-library dependencies are properly supported by the dynamic linker, for example, on DEC OSF/1 3 and 4.

'`none`'   It causes deplibs to be reassigned '`deplibs=""`'. That way '`archive_cmds`' can contain deplibs on all platforms, but not have deplibs used unless needed.

'`unknown`' is the default for all systems unless overridden in `libtool.m4`. It is the same as '`none`', but it documents that we really don't know what the correct value should be, and we welcome patches that improve it.

Then in `ltmain.in` we have the real workhorse: a little initialization and postprocessing (to setup/release variables for use with eval echo libname_spec etc.) and a case statement that decides the method that is being used. This is the real code... I wish I could condense it a little more, but I don't think I can without function calls. I've mostly optimized it (moved things out of loops, etc.) but there is probably some fat left. I thought I should stop while I was ahead, work on whatever bugs you discover, etc. before thinking about more than obvious optimizations.

15.2 Tested platforms

This table describes when libtool was last known to be tested on platforms where it claims
to support shared libraries:

```
-------------------------------------------------------
canonical host name          compiler  libtool results
  (tools versions)                     release
-------------------------------------------------------
alpha-dec-osf5.1 cc   1.3e   ok (1.910)
alpha-dec-osf4.0f            gcc       1.3e    ok (1.910)
alpha-dec-osf4.0f            cc        1.3e    ok (1.910)
alpha-dec-osf3.2            gcc       0.8     ok
alpha-dec-osf3.2            cc        0.8     ok
alpha-dec-osf2.1            gcc       1.2f    NS
alpha*-unknown-linux-gnu    gcc       1.3b    ok
  (egcs-1.1.2, GNU ld 2.9.1.0.23)
hppa2.0w-hp-hpux11.00       cc        1.2f    ok
hppa2.0-hp-hpux10.20        cc        1.3.2   ok
hppa1.1-hp-hpux10.20        gcc       1.2f    ok
hppa1.1-hp-hpux10.20        cc        1.3c    ok (1.821)
hppa1.1-hp-hpux10.10        gcc       1.2f    ok
hppa1.1-hp-hpux10.10        cc        1.2f    ok
hppa1.1-hp-hpux9.07         gcc       1.2f    ok
hppa1.1-hp-hpux9.07         cc        1.2f    ok
hppa1.1-hp-hpux9.05         gcc       1.2f    ok
hppa1.1-hp-hpux9.05         cc        1.2f    ok
hppa1.1-hp-hpux9.01         gcc       1.2f    ok
hppa1.1-hp-hpux9.01         cc        1.2f    ok
i*86-*-beos                 gcc       1.2f    ok
i*86-*-bsdi4.0.1            gcc       1.3c    ok
  (gcc-2.7.2.1)
i*86-*-bsdi4.0              gcc       1.2f    ok
i*86-*-bsdi3.1              gcc       1.2e    NS
i*86-*-bsdi3.0              gcc       1.2e    NS
i*86-*-bsdi2.1              gcc       1.2e    NS
i*86-pc-cygwin              gcc       1.3b    NS
  (egcs-1.1 stock b20.1 compiler)
i*86-*-dguxR4.20MU01        gcc       1.2     ok
i*86-*-freebsd4.3 gcc       1.3e      ok (1.912)
i*86-*-freebsdelf4.0        gcc       1.3c    ok
  (egcs-1.1.2)
i*86-*-freebsdelf3.2        gcc       1.3c    ok
  (gcc-2.7.2.1)
i*86-*-freebsdelf3.1        gcc       1.3c    ok
  (gcc-2.7.2.1)
i*86-*-freebsdelf3.0        gcc       1.3c    ok
i*86-*-freebsd3.0           gcc       1.2e    ok
```

```
i*86-*-freebsd2.2.8              gcc      1.3c     ok
  (gcc-2.7.2.1)
i*86-*-freebsd2.2.6              gcc      1.3b     ok
  (egcs-1.1 & gcc-2.7.2.1, native ld)
i*86-*-freebsd2.1.5              gcc      0.5      ok
i*86-*-netbsd1.5                 gcc      1.3e     ok (1.901)
  (egcs-1.1.2)
i*86-*-netbsd1.4                 gcc      1.3c     ok
  (egcs-1.1.1)
i*86-*-netbsd1.4.3A              gcc      1.3e     ok (1.901)
i*86-*-netbsd1.3.3               gcc      1.3c     ok
  (gcc-2.7.2.2+myc2)
i*86-*-netbsd1.3.2               gcc      1.2e     ok
i*86-*-netbsd1.3I                gcc      1.2e     ok
  (egcs 1.1?)
i*86-*-netbsd1.2                 gcc      0.9g     ok
i*86-*-linux-gnu gcc  1.3e   ok (1.901)
  (Red Hat 7.0, gcc "2.96")
i*86-*-linux-gnu gcc  1.3e   ok (1.911)
  (SuSE 7.0, gcc 2.95.2)
i*86-*-linux-gnulibc1            gcc      1.2f     ok
i*86-*-openbsd2.5                gcc      1.3c     ok
  (gcc-2.8.1)
i*86-*-openbsd2.4                gcc      1.3c     ok
  (gcc-2.8.1)
i*86-*-solaris2.7                gcc      1.3b     ok
  (egcs-1.1.2, native ld)
i*86-*-solaris2.6                gcc      1.2f     ok
i*86-*-solaris2.5.1              gcc      1.2f     ok
i*86-ncr-sysv4.3.03              gcc      1.2f     ok
i*86-ncr-sysv4.3.03              cc       1.2e     ok
  (cc -Hnocopyr)
i*86-pc-sco3.2v5.0.5 cc  1.3c   ok
i*86-pc-sco3.2v5.0.5 gcc  1.3c   ok
  (gcc 95q4c)
i*86-pc-sco3.2v5.0.5 gcc  1.3c   ok
  (egcs-1.1.2)
i*86-sco-sysv5uw7.1.1 gcc  1.3e   ok (1.901)
  (gcc-2.95.2, SCO linker)
i*86-UnixWare7.1.0-sysv5 cc  1.3c    ok
i*86-UnixWare7.1.0-sysv5 gcc  1.3c    ok
  (egcs-1.1.1)
m68k-next-nextstep3              gcc      1.2f     NS
m68k-sun-sunos4.1.1              gcc      1.2f     NS
  (gcc-2.5.7)
m88k-dg-dguxR4.12TMU01           gcc      1.2      ok
m88k-motorola-sysv4              gcc      1.3      ok
```

```
  (egcs-1.1.2)
mips-sgi-irix6.5              gcc     1.2f    ok
  (gcc-2.8.1)
mips-sgi-irix6.4             gcc     1.2f    ok
mips-sgi-irix6.3             gcc     1.3b    ok
  (egcs-1.1.2, native ld)
mips-sgi-irix6.3             cc      1.3b    ok
  (cc 7.0)
mips-sgi-irix6.2             gcc     1.2f    ok
mips-sgi-irix6.2             cc      0.9     ok
mips-sgi-irix5.3             gcc     1.2f    ok
  (egcs-1.1.1)
mips-sgi-irix5.3             gcc     1.2f    NS
  (gcc-2.6.3)
mips-sgi-irix5.3             cc      0.8     ok
mips-sgi-irix5.2             gcc     1.3b    ok
  (egcs-1.1.2, native ld)
mips-sgi-irix5.2             cc      1.3b    ok
  (cc 3.10)
mips-sni-sysv4 cc       1.3.5    ok
  (Siemens C-compiler)
mips-sni-sysv4 gcc      1.3.5    ok
  (gcc-2.7.2.3, GNU assembler 2.8.1, native ld)
mipsel-unknown-openbsd2.1    gcc     1.0     ok
powerpc-apple-darwin6.4      gcc     1.5     ok
(apple dev tools released 12/2002)
powerpc-ibm-aix4.3.1.0       gcc     1.2f    ok
  (egcs-1.1.1)
powerpc-ibm-aix4.2.1.0       gcc     1.2f    ok
  (egcs-1.1.1)
powerpc-ibm-aix4.1.5.0       gcc     1.2f    ok
  (egcs-1.1.1)
powerpc-ibm-aix4.1.5.0       gcc     1.2f    NS
  (gcc-2.8.1)
powerpc-ibm-aix4.1.4.0       gcc     1.0     ok
powerpc-ibm-aix4.1.4.0       xlc     1.0i    ok
rs6000-ibm-aix4.1.5.0        gcc     1.2f    ok
  (gcc-2.7.2)
rs6000-ibm-aix4.1.4.0        gcc     1.2f    ok
  (gcc-2.7.2)
rs6000-ibm-aix3.2.5          gcc     1.0i    ok
rs6000-ibm-aix3.2.5          xlc     1.0i    ok
sparc-sun-solaris2.8 gcc  1.3e   ok (1.913)
  (gcc-2.95.3 & native ld)
sparc-sun-solaris2.7         gcc     1.3e    ok (1.913)
  (gcc-2.95.3 & native ld)
sparc-sun-solaris2.6         gcc     1.3e    ok (1.913)
```

```
    (gcc-2.95.3 & native ld)
  sparc-sun-solaris2.5.1          gcc      1.3e     ok (1.911)
  sparc-sun-solaris2.5            gcc      1.3b     ok
    (egcs-1.1.2, GNU ld 2.9.1 & native ld)
  sparc-sun-solaris2.5            cc       1.3b     ok
    (SC 3.0.1)
  sparc-sun-solaris2.4            gcc      1.0a     ok
  sparc-sun-solaris2.4            cc       1.0a     ok
  sparc-sun-solaris2.3            gcc      1.2f     ok
  sparc-sun-sunos4.1.4            gcc      1.2f     ok
  sparc-sun-sunos4.1.4            cc       1.0f     ok
  sparc-sun-sunos4.1.3_U1         gcc      1.2f     ok
  sparc-sun-sunos4.1.3C           gcc      1.2f     ok
  sparc-sun-sunos4.1.3            gcc      1.3b     ok
    (egcs-1.1.2, GNU ld 2.9.1 & native ld)
  sparc-sun-sunos4.1.3            cc       1.3b     ok
  sparc-unknown-bsdi4.0           gcc      1.2c     ok
  sparc-unknown-linux-gnulibc1    gcc      1.2f     ok
  sparc-unknown-linux-gnu         gcc      1.3b     ok
    (egcs-1.1.2, GNU ld 2.9.1.0.23)
  sparc64-unknown-linux-gnu       gcc      1.2f     ok

Notes:
- "ok" means "all tests passed".
- "NS" means "Not Shared", but OK for static libraries
```

Note: The vendor-distributed HP-UX sed(1) programs are horribly broken, and cannot handle libtool's requirements, so users may report unusual problems. There is no workaround except to install a working sed (such as GNU sed) on these systems.

Note: The vendor-distributed NCR MP-RAS cc programs emits copyright on standard error that confuse tests on size of conftest.err. The workaround is to specify CC when run configure with CC='cc -Hnocopyr'.

15.3 Platform quirks

This section is dedicated to the sanity of the libtool maintainers. It describes the programs that libtool uses, how they vary from system to system, and how to test for them.

Because libtool is a shell script, it can be difficult to understand just by reading it from top to bottom. This section helps show why libtool does things a certain way. Combined with the scripts themselves, you should have a better sense of how to improve libtool, or write your own.

15.3.1 References

The following is a list of valuable documentation references:

- SGI's IRIX Manual Pages can be found at
  http://techpubs.sgi.com/cgi-bin/infosrch.cgi?cmd=browse&db=man.

- Sun's free service area (`http://www.sun.com/service/online/free.html`) and documentation server (`http://docs.sun.com/`).

- Compaq's Tru64 UNIX online documentation is at (`http://tru64unix.compaq.com/faqs/publications/pub_page/doc_list.html`) with C++ documentation at (`http://tru64unix.compaq.com/cplus/docs/index.htm`).

- Hewlett-Packard has online documentation at (`http://docs.hp.com/index.html`).

- IBM has online documentation at (`http://www.rs6000.ibm.com/resource/aix_resource/Pubs/`).

15.3.2 Compilers

The only compiler characteristics that affect libtool are the flags needed (if any) to generate PIC objects. In general, if a C compiler supports certain PIC flags, then any derivative compilers support the same flags. Until there are some noteworthy exceptions to this rule, this section will document only C compilers.

The following C compilers have standard command line options, regardless of the platform:

`gcc`

> This is the GNU C compiler, which is also the system compiler for many free operating systems (FreeBSD, GNU/Hurd, GNU/Linux, Lites, NetBSD, and OpenBSD, to name a few).
>
> The `-fpic` or `-fPIC` flags can be used to generate position-independent code. `-fPIC` is guaranteed to generate working code, but the code is slower on m68k, m88k, and SPARC chips. However, using `-fpic` on those chips imposes arbitrary size limits on the shared libraries.

The rest of this subsection lists compilers by the operating system that they are bundled with:

`aix3*`

`aix4*`   Most AIX compilers have no PIC flags, since AIX (with the exception of AIX for IA-64) runs on PowerPC and RS/6000 chips.[1]

`hpux10*`   Use '+Z' to generate PIC.

`osf3*`   Digital/UNIX 3.x does not have PIC flags, at least not on the PowerPC platform.

`solaris2*`
     Use `-KPIC` to generate PIC.

`sunos4*`   Use `-PIC` to generate PIC.

---

[1] All code compiled for the PowerPC and RS/6000 chips (`powerpc-*-*`, `powerpcle-*-*`, and `rs6000-*-*`) is position-independent, regardless of the operating system or compiler suite. So, "regular objects" can be used to build shared libraries on these systems and no special PIC compiler flags are required.

15.3.3 Reloadable objects

On all known systems, a reloadable object can be created by running `ld -r -o output.o input1.o input2.o`. This reloadable object may be treated as exactly equivalent to other objects.

15.3.4 Multiple dependencies

On most modern platforms the order where dependent libraries are listed has no effect on object generation. In theory, there are platforms that require libraries that provide missing symbols to other libraries to be listed after those libraries whose symbols they provide.

Particularly, if a pair of static archives each resolve some of the other's symbols, it might be necessary to list one of those archives both before and after the other one. Libtool does not currently cope with this situation well, since duplicate libraries are removed from the link line by default. Libtool provides the command line option `--preserve-dup-deps` to preserve all duplicate dependencies in cases where it is necessary.

15.3.5 Archivers

On all known systems, building a static library can be accomplished by running `ar cru libname.a obj1.o obj2.o ...`, where the `.a` file is the output library, and each `.o` file is an object file.

On all known systems, if there is a program named `ranlib`, then it must be used to "bless" the created library before linking against it, with the `ranlib libname.a` command. Some systems, like Irix, use the `ar ts` command, instead.

15.3.6 Cross compiling

Most build systems support the ability to compile libraries and applications on one platform for use on a different platform, provided a compiler capable of generating the appropriate output is available. In such cross compiling scenarios, the platform where the libraries or applications are compiled is called the *build platform*, while the platform where the libraries or applications are intended to be used or executed is called the *host platform*. Section "The GNU Build System" in *The Automake Manual*, of which libtool is a part, supports cross compiling via arguments passed to the configure script: `--build=...` and `--host=....` However, when the build platform and host platform are very different, libtool is required to make certain accommodations to support these scenarios.

In most cases, because the build platform and host platform differ, the cross-compiled libraries and executables can't be executed or tested on the build platform where they were compiled. The testsuites of most build systems will often skip any tests that involve executing such foreign executables when cross-compiling. However, if the build platform and host platform are sufficiently similar, it is often possible to run cross-compiled applications. Libtool's own testsuite often attempts to execute cross-compiled tests, but will mark any failures as *skipped* since the failure might simply be due to the differences between the two platforms.

In addition to cases where the host platform and build platform are extremely similar (e.g. 'i586-pc-linux-gnu' and 'i686-pc-linux-gnu'), there is another case where cross-compiled host applications may be executed on the build platform. This is possible when the build platform supports an emulation or API-enhanced environment for the host platform.

One example of this situation would be if the build platform were MinGW, and the host platform were Cygwin (or vice versa). Both of these platforms can actually operate within a single Windows instance, so Cygwin applications can be launched from a MinGW context, and vice versa—provided certain care is taken. Another example would be if the build platform were GNU/Linux on an x86 32bit processor, and the host platform were MinGW. In this situation, the Wine (`http://www.winehq.org/`) environment can be used to launch Windows applications from the GNU/Linux operating system; again, provided certain care is taken.

One particular issue occurs when a Windows platform such as MinGW, Cygwin, or MSYS is the host or build platform, while the other platform is a Unix-style system. In these cases, there are often conflicts between the format of the file names and paths expected within host platform libraries and executables, and those employed on the build platform.

This situation is best described using a concrete example: suppose the build platform is GNU/Linux with canonical triplet '`i686-pc-linux-gnu`'. Suppose further that the host platform is MinGW with canonical triplet '`i586-pc-mingw32`'. On the GNU/Linux platform there is a cross compiler following the usual naming conventions of such compilers, where the compiler name is prefixed by the host canonical triplet (or suitable alias). (For more information concerning canonical triplets and platform aliases, see Section "Specifying Target Triplets" in *The Autoconf Manual* and Section "Canonicalizing" in *The Autoconf Manual*) In this case, the C compiler is named '`i586-pc-mingw32-gcc`'.

As described in Section 3.3.1 [Wrapper executables], page 9, for the MinGW host platform libtool uses a wrapper executable to set various environment variables before launching the actual program executable. Like the program executable, the wrapper executable is cross-compiled for the host platform (that is, for MinGW). As described above, ordinarily a host platform executable cannot be executed on the build platform, but in this case the Wine environment could be used to launch the MinGW application from GNU/Linux. However, the wrapper executable, as a host platform (MinGW) application, must set the `PATH` variable so that the true application's dependent libraries can be located—but the contents of the `PATH` variable must be structured for MinGW. Libtool must use the Wine file name mapping facilities to determine the correct value so that the wrapper executable can set the `PATH` variable to point to the correct location.

For example, suppose we are compiling an application in `/var/tmp` on GNU/Linux, using separate source code and build directories:

`/var/tmp/foo-1.2.3/app/`	(application source code)
`/var/tmp/foo-1.2.3/lib/`	(library source code)
`/var/tmp/BUILD/app/`	(application build objects here)
`/var/tmp/BUILD/lib/`	(library build objects here)

Since the library will be built in `/var/tmp/BUILD/lib`, the wrapper executable (which will be in `/var/tmp/BUILD/app`) must add that directory to `PATH` (actually, it must add the directory named *objdir* under `/var/tmp/BUILD/lib`, but we'll ignore that detail for now). However, Windows does not have a concept of Unix-style file or directory names such as `/var/tmp/BUILD/lib`. Therefore, Wine provides a mapping from Windows file names such as `C:\Program Files` to specific Unix-style file names. Wine also provides a utility that can be used to map Unix-style file names to Windows file names.

In this case, the wrapper executable should actually add the value

```
Z:\var\tmp\BUILD\lib
```

to the `PATH`. libtool contains support for path conversions of this type, for a certain limited set of build and host platform combinations. In this case, libtool will invoke Wine's `winepath` utility to ensure that the correct `PATH` value is used. See Section 15.3.7 [File name conversion], page 93.

15.3.7 File name conversion

In certain situations, libtool must convert file names and paths between formats appropriate to different platforms. Usually this occurs when cross-compiling, and affects only the ability to launch host platform executables on the build platform using an emulation or API-enhancement environment such as Wine. Failure to convert paths (see Section 15.3.7.1 [File Name Conversion Failure], page 94) will cause a warning to be issued, but rarely causes the build to fail—and should have no affect on the compiled products, once installed properly on the host platform. For more information, see Section 15.3.6 [Cross compiling], page 91.

However, file name conversion may also occur in another scenario: when using a Unix emulation system on Windows (such as Cygwin or MSYS), combined with a native Windows compiler such as MinGW or MSVC. Only a limited set of such scenarios are currently supported; in other cases file name conversion is skipped. The lack of file name conversion usually means that uninstalled executables can't be launched, but only rarely causes the build to fail (see Section 15.3.7.1 [File Name Conversion Failure], page 94).

libtool supports file name conversion in the following scenarios:

build platform	host platform	Notes
MinGW (MSYS)	MinGW (Windows)	see Section 15.3.7.2 [Native MinGW File Name Conversion], page 94
Cygwin	MinGW (Windows)	see Section 15.3.7.3 [Cygwin/Windows File Name Conversion], page 94
Unix + Wine	MinGW (Windows)	Requires Wine. See Section 15.3.7.4 [Unix/Windows File Name Conversion], page 95.
MinGW (MSYS)	Cygwin	Requires `LT_CYGPATH`. See Section 15.3.7.5 [LT_CYGPATH], page 95. Provided for testing purposes only.
Unix + Wine	Cygwin	Requires both Wine and `LT_CYGPATH`, but does not yet work with Cygwin 1.7.7 and Wine-1.2. See Section 15.3.7.4 [Unix/Windows File Name Conversion], page 95, and Section 15.3.7.5 [LT_CYGPATH], page 95.

15.3.7.1 File Name Conversion Failure

In most cases, file name conversion is not needed or attempted. However, when libtool detects that a specific combination of build and host platform does require file name conversion, it is possible that the conversion may fail. In these cases, you may see a warning such as the following:

```
Could not determine the host file name corresponding to
  '... a file name ...'
Continuing, but uninstalled executables may not work.
```

or

```
Could not determine the host path corresponding to
  '... a path ...'
Continuing, but uninstalled executables may not work.
```

This should not cause the build to fail. At worst, it means that the wrapper executable will specify file names or paths appropriate for the build platform. Since those are not appropriate for the host platform, the uninstalled executables would not operate correctly, even when the wrapper executable is launched via the appropriate emulation or API-enhancement (e.g. Wine). Simply install the executables on the host platform, and execute them there.

15.3.7.2 Native MinGW File Name Conversion

MSYS is a Unix emulation environment for Windows, and is specifically designed such that in normal usage it *pretends* to be MinGW or native Windows, but understands Unix-style file names and paths, and supports standard Unix tools and shells. Thus, "native" MinGW builds are actually an odd sort of cross-compile, from an MSYS Unix emulation environment "pretending" to be MinGW, to actual native Windows.

When an MSYS shell launches a native Windows executable (as opposed to other *MSYS* executables), it uses a system of heuristics to detect any command-line arguments that contain file names or paths. It automatically converts these file names from the MSYS (Unix-like) format, to the corresponding Windows file name, before launching the executable. However, this auto-conversion facility is only available when using the MSYS runtime library. The wrapper executable itself is a MinGW application (that is, it does not use the MSYS runtime library). The wrapper executable must set `PATH` to, and call `_spawnv` with, values that have already been converted from MSYS format to Windows. Thus, when libtool writes the source code for the wrapper executable, it must manually convert MSYS paths to Windows format, so that the Windows values can be hard-coded into the wrapper executable.

15.3.7.3 Cygwin/Windows File Name Conversion

Cygwin provides a Unix emulation environment for Windows. As part of that emulation, it provides a file system mapping that presents the Windows file system in a Unix-compatible manner. Cygwin also provides a utility `cygpath` that can be used to convert file names and paths between the two representations. In a correctly configured Cygwin installation, `cygpath` is always present, and is in the `PATH`.

Libtool uses `cygpath` to convert from Cygwin (Unix-style) file names and paths to Windows format when the build platform is Cygwin and the host platform is MinGW.

When the host platform is Cygwin, but the build platform is MSYS or some Unix system, libtool also uses `cygpath` to convert from Windows to Cygwin format (after first converting from the build platform format to Windows format; See Section 15.3.7.2 [Native MinGW File Name Conversion], page 94, and Section 15.3.7.4 [Unix/Windows File Name Conversion], page 95.) Because the build platform is not Cygwin, `cygpath` is not (and should not be) in the `PATH`. Therefore, in this configuration the environment variable `LT_CYGPATH` is required. See Section 15.3.7.5 [LT_CYGPATH], page 95.

15.3.7.4 Unix/Windows File Name Conversion

Wine (`http://www.winehq.org/`) provides an interpretation environment for some Unix platforms where Windows applications can be executed. It provides a mapping between the Unix file system and a virtual Windows file system used by the Windows programs. For the file name conversion to work, Wine must be installed and properly configured on the build platform, and the `winepath` application must be in the build platform's `PATH`. In addition, on 32bit GNU/Linux it is usually helpful if the binfmt extension is enabled.

15.3.7.5 LT_CYGPATH

For some cross-compile configurations (where the host platform is Cygwin), the `cygpath` program is used to convert file names from the build platform notation to the Cygwin form (technically, this conversion is from Windows notation to Cygwin notation; the conversion from the build platform format to Windows notation is performed via other means). However, because the `cygpath` program is not (and should not be) in the `PATH` on the build platform, `LT_CYGPATH` must specify the full build platform file name (that is, the full Unix or MSYS file name) of the `cygpath` program.

The reason `cygpath` should not be in the build platform `PATH` is twofold: first, `cygpath` is usually installed in the same directory as many other Cygwin executables, such as `sed`, `cp`, etc. If the build platform environment had this directory in its `PATH`, then these Cygwin versions of common Unix utilities might be used in preference to the ones provided by the build platform itself, with deleterious effects. Second, especially when Cygwin-1.7 or later is used, multiple Cygwin installations can coexist within the same Windows instance. Each installation will have separate "mount tables" specified in `CYGROOT-N/etc/fstab`. These *mount tables* control how that instance of Cygwin will map Windows file names and paths to Cygwin form. Each installation's `cygpath` utility automatically deduces the appropriate `/etc/fstab` file. Since each `CYGROOT-N/etc/fstab` mount table may specify different mappings, it matters what `cygpath` is used.

Note that `cygpath` is a Cygwin application; to execute this tool from Unix requires a working and properly configured Wine installation, as well as enabling the GNU/Linux `binfmt` extension. Furthermore, the Cygwin `setup.exe` tool should have been used, via Wine, to properly install Cygwin into the Wine file system (and registry).

Unfortunately, Wine support for Cygwin is intermittent. Recent releases of Cygwin (1.7 and above) appear to require more Windows API support than Wine provides (as of Wine version 1.2); most Cygwin applications fail to execute. This includes `cygpath` itself. Hence, it is best *not* to use the LT_CYGPATH machinery in libtool when performing Unix to Cygwin cross-compiles. Similarly, it is best *not* to enable the GNU/Linux binfmt support in this configuration, because while Wine will fail to execute the compiled Cygwin applications, it will still exit with status zero. This tends to confuse build systems and test suites (including libtool's own testsuite, resulting in spurious reported failures). Wine support for the older Cygwin-1.5 series appears satisfactory, but the Cygwin team no longer supports Cygwin-1.5. It is hoped that Wine will eventually be improved such that Cygwin-1.7 will again operate correctly under Wine. Until then, libtool will report warnings as described in see Section 15.3.7.1 [File Name Conversion Failure], page 94 in these scenarios.

However, `LT_CYGPATH` is also used for the MSYS to Cygwin cross compile scenario, and operates as expected.

15.3.7.6 Cygwin to MinGW Cross

There are actually three different scenarios that could all legitimately be called a "Cygwin to MinGW" cross compile. The current (and standard) definition is when there is a compiler that produces native Windows libraries and applications, but which itself is a Cygwin application, just as would be expected in any other cross compile setup.

However, historically there were two other definitions, which we will refer to as the *fake* one, and the *lying* one.

In the *fake* Cygwin to MinGW cross compile case, you actually use a native MinGW compiler, but you do so from within a Cygwin environment:

```
export PATH="/c/MinGW/bin:${PATH}"
configure --build=i686-pc-cygwin \
--host=mingw32 \
NM=/c/MinGW/bin/nm.exe
```

In this way, the build system "knows" that you are cross compiling, and the file name conversion logic will be used. However, because the tools (`mingw32-gcc`, `nm`, `ar`) used are actually native Windows applications, they will not understand any Cygwin (that is, Unix-like) absolute file names passed as command line arguments (and, unlike MSYS, Cygwin does not automatically convert such arguments). However, so long as only relative file names are used in the build system, and non-Windows-supported Unix idioms such as symlinks and mount points are avoided, this scenario should work.

If you must use absolute file names, you will have to force Libtool to convert file names for the toolchain in this case, by doing the following before you run configure:

```
export lt_cv_to_tool_file_cmd=func_convert_file_cygwin_to_w32
```

In the *lying* Cygwin to MinGW cross compile case, you lie to the build system:

```
export PATH="/c/MinGW/bin:${PATH}"
configure --build=i686-pc-mingw32 \
--host=i686-pc-mingw32 \
--disable-dependency-tracking
```

and claim that the build platform is MinGW, even though you are actually running under *Cygwin* and not MinGW. In this case, libtool does *not* know that you are performing a cross compile, and thinks instead that you are performing a native MinGW build. However, as described in (see Section 15.3.7.2 [Native MinGW File Name Conversion], page 94), that scenario triggers an "MSYS to Windows" file name conversion. This, of course, is the wrong conversion since we are actually running under Cygwin. Also, the toolchain is expecting Windows file names (not Cygwin) but unless told so Libtool will feed Cygwin file names to the toolchain in this case. To force the correct file name conversions in this situation, you should do the following *before* running configure:

```
export lt_cv_to_host_file_cmd=func_convert_file_cygwin_to_w32
export lt_cv_to_tool_file_cmd=func_convert_file_cygwin_to_w32
```

Note that this relies on internal implementation details of libtool, and is subject to change. Also, --disable-dependency-tracking is required, because otherwise the MinGW GCC will generate dependency files that contain Windows file names. This, in turn, will confuse the Cygwin make program, which does not accept Windows file names:

```
Makefile:1: *** target pattern contains no '%'.  Stop.
```

There have also always been a number of other details required for the *lying* case to operate correctly, such as the use of so-called *identity mounts*:

```
# cygwin-root/etc/fstab
D:/foo    /foo     some_fs binary 0 0
D:/bar    /bar     some_fs binary 0 0
E:/grill  /grill   some_fs binary 0 0
```

In this way, top-level directories of each drive are available using identical names within Cygwin.

Note that you also need to ensure that the standard Unix directories (like /bin, /lib, /usr, /etc) appear in the root of a drive. This means that you must install Cygwin itself into the C:/ root directory (or D:/, or E:/, etc)—instead of the recommended installation into C:/cygwin/. In addition, all file names used in the build system must be relative, symlinks should not be used within the source or build directory trees, and all -M* options to gcc except -MMD must be avoided.

This is quite a fragile setup, but it has been in historical use, and so is documented here.

15.3.8 Windows DLLs

This topic describes a couple of ways to portably create Windows Dynamic Link Libraries (DLLs). Libtool knows how to create DLLs using GNU tools and using Microsoft tools.

A typical library has a "hidden" implementation with an interface described in a header file. On just about every system, the interface could be something like this:

Example foo.h:

```
#ifndef FOO_H
#define FOO_H

int one (void);
int two (void);
extern int three;

#endif /* FOO_H */
```

And the implementation could be something like this:

Example foo.c:

```
#include "foo.h"

int one (void)
{
  return 1;
```

```
}

int two (void)
{
  return three - one ();
}

int three = 3;
```

When using contemporary GNU tools to create the Windows DLL, the above code will work there too, thanks to its auto-import/auto-export features. But that is not the case when using older GNU tools or perhaps more interestingly when using proprietary tools. In those cases the code will need additional decorations on the interface symbols with `_ _declspec(dllimport)` and `__declspec(dllexport)` depending on whether the library is built or it's consumed and how it's built and consumed. However, it should be noted that it would have worked also with Microsoft tools, if only the variable **three** hadn't been there, due to the fact the Microsoft tools will automatically import functions (but sadly not variables) and Libtool will automatically export non-static symbols as described next.

With Microsoft tools, Libtool digs through the object files that make up the library, looking for non-static symbols to automatically export. I.e., Libtool with Microsoft tools tries to mimic the auto-export feature of contemporary GNU tools. It should be noted that the GNU auto-export feature is turned off when an explicit `__declspec(dllexport)` is seen. The GNU tools do this to not make more symbols visible for projects that have already taken the trouble to decorate symbols. There is no similar way to limit what symbols are visible in the code when Libtool is using Microsoft tools. In order to limit symbol visibility in that case you need to use one of the options `-export-symbols` or `-export-symbols-regex`.

No matching help with auto-import is provided by Libtool, which is why variables must be decorated to import them from a DLL for everything but contemporary GNU tools. As stated above, functions are automatically imported by both contemporary GNU tools and Microsoft tools, but for other proprietary tools the auto-import status of functions is unknown.

When the objects that form the library are built, there are generally two copies built for each object. One copy is used when linking the DLL and one copy is used for the static library. On Windows systems, a pair of defines are commonly used to discriminate how the interface symbols should be decorated. The first define is '`-DDLL_EXPORT`', which is automatically provided by Libtool when **libtool** builds the copy of the object that is destined for the DLL. The second define is '`-DLIBFOO_BUILD`' (or similar), which is often added by the package providing the library and is used when building the library, but not when consuming the library.

However, the matching double compile is not performed when consuming libraries. It is therefore not possible to reliably distinguish if the consumer is importing from a DLL or if it is going to use a static library.

With contemporary GNU tools, auto-import often saves the day, but see the GNU ld documentation and its `--enable-auto-import` option for some corner cases when it does not (see Section "Options specific to i386 PE targets" in *Using ld, the GNU linker*).

With Microsoft tools you typically get away with always compiling the code such that variables are expected to be imported from a DLL and functions are expected to be found in a static library. The tools will then automatically import the function from a DLL if that is where they are found. If the variables are not imported from a DLL as expected, but are found in a static library that is otherwise pulled in by some function, the linker will issue a warning (LNK4217) that a locally defined symbol is imported, but it still works. In other words, this scheme will not work to only consume variables from a library. There is also a price connected to this liberal use of imports in that an extra indirection is introduced when you are consuming the static version of the library. That extra indirection is unavoidable when the DLL is consumed, but it is not needed when consuming the static library.

For older GNU tools and other proprietary tools there is no generic way to make it possible to consume either of the DLL or the static library without user intervention, the tools need to be told what is intended. One common assumption is that if a DLL is being built ('DLL_EXPORT' is defined) then that DLL is going to consume any dependent libraries as DLLs. If that assumption is made everywhere, it is possible to select how an end-user application is consuming libraries by adding a single flag '-DDLL_EXPORT' when a DLL build is required. This is of course an all or nothing deal, either everything as DLLs or everything as static libraries.

To sum up the above, the header file of the foo library needs to be changed into something like this:

Modified `foo.h`:

```
#ifndef FOO_H
#define FOO_H

#if defined _WIN32 && !defined __GNUC__
# ifdef LIBFOO_BUILD
#  ifdef DLL_EXPORT
#   define LIBFOO_SCOPE              __declspec (dllexport)
#   define LIBFOO_SCOPE_VAR extern __declspec (dllexport)
#  endif
# elif defined _MSC_VER
#  define LIBFOO_SCOPE
#  define LIBFOO_SCOPE_VAR  extern __declspec (dllimport)
# elif defined DLL_EXPORT
#  define LIBFOO_SCOPE              __declspec (dllimport)
#  define LIBFOO_SCOPE_VAR  extern __declspec (dllimport)
# endif
#endif
#ifndef LIBFOO_SCOPE
# define LIBFOO_SCOPE
# define LIBFOO_SCOPE_VAR extern
#endif

LIBFOO_SCOPE     int one (void);
LIBFOO_SCOPE     int two (void);
LIBFOO_SCOPE_VAR int three;
```

```
#endif /* FOO_H */
```

When the targets are limited to contemporary GNU tools and Microsoft tools, the above can be simplified to the following:

Simplified `foo.h`:

```
#ifndef FOO_H
#define FOO_H

#if defined _WIN32 && !defined __GNUC__ && !defined LIBFOO_BUILD
# define LIBFOO_SCOPE_VAR extern __declspec (dllimport)
#else
# define LIBFOO_SCOPE_VAR extern
#endif

int one (void);
int two (void);
LIBFOO_SCOPE_VAR int three;

#endif /* FOO_H */
```

This last simplified version can of course only work when Libtool is used to build the DLL, as no symbols would be exported otherwise (i.e., when using Microsoft tools).

It should be noted that there are various projects that attempt to relax these requirements by various low level tricks, but they are not discussed here. Examples are FlexDLL (`http://alain.frisch.fr/flexdll.html`) and edll (`http://edll.sourceforge.net/`).

15.4 `libtool` script contents

Since version 1.4, the `libtool` script is generated by **configure** (see Section 5.4 [Configuring], page 27). In earlier versions, **configure** achieved this by calling a helper script called `ltconfig`. From libtool version 0.7 to 1.0, this script simply set shell variables, then sourced the libtool backend, `ltmain.sh`. `ltconfig` from libtool version 1.1 through 1.3 inlined the contents of `ltmain.sh` into the generated `libtool`, which improved performance on many systems. The tests that `ltconfig` used to perform are now kept in `libtool.m4` where they can be written using Autoconf. This has the runtime performance benefits of inlined `ltmain.sh`, *and* improves the build time a little while considerably easing the amount of raw shell code that used to need maintaining.

The convention used for naming variables that hold shell commands for delayed evaluation, is to use the suffix `_cmd` where a single line of valid shell script is needed, and the suffix `_cmds` where multiple lines of shell script **may** be delayed for later evaluation. By convention, `_cmds` variables delimit the evaluation units with the ~ character where necessary.

Here is a listing of each of the configuration variables, and how they are used within `ltmain.sh` (see Section 5.4 [Configuring], page 27):

`AR`   [Variable]
          The name of the system library archiver.

CC   [Variable]
> The name of the compiler used to configure libtool. This will always contain the
> compiler for the current language (see Section 6.2 [Tags], page 39).

ECHO   [Variable]
> An `echo` program that does not interpret backslashes as an escape character. It may
> be given only one argument, so due quoting is necessary.

LD   [Variable]
> The name of the linker that libtool should use internally for reloadable linking and
> possibly shared libraries.

LTCC   [Variable]
LTCFLAGS   [Variable]
> The name of the C compiler and C compiler flags used to configure libtool.

NM   [Variable]
> The name of a BSD- or MS-compatible program that produces listings of global
> symbols. For BSD `nm`, the symbols should be in one the following formats:
>
> ```
> address C global-variable-name
> address D global-variable-name
> address T global-function-name
> ```
>
> For MS `dumpbin`, the symbols should be in one of the following formats:
>
> ```
> counter size     UNDEF    notype        External    | global-var
> counter address section  notype        External    | global-var
> counter address section  notype ()     External    | global-func
> ```
>
> The *size* of the global variables are not zero and the *section* of the global functions are
> not "UNDEF". Symbols in "pick any" sections ("pick any" appears in the section
> header) are not global either.

RANLIB   [Variable]
> Set to the name of the `ranlib` program, if any.

allow_undefined_flag   [Variable]
> The flag that is used by 'archive_cmds' to declare that there will be unresolved
> symbols in the resulting shared library. Empty, if no such flag is required. Set
> to 'unsupported' if there is no way to generate a shared library with references to
> symbols that aren't defined in that library.

always_export_symbols   [Variable]
> Whether libtool should automatically generate a list of exported symbols using
> `export_symbols_cmds` before linking an archive. Set to 'yes' or 'no'. Default is 'no'.

archive_cmds   [Variable]
archive_expsym_cmds   [Variable]
old_archive_cmds   [Variable]
> Commands used to create shared libraries, shared libraries with **-export-symbols**
> and static libraries, respectively.

`archiver_list_spec` [Variable]

Specify filename containing input files for **AR**.

`old_archive_from_new_cmds` [Variable]

If the shared library depends on a static library, 'old_archive_from_new_cmds' contains the commands used to create that static library. If this variable is not empty, 'old_archive_cmds' is not used.

`old_archive_from_expsyms_cmds` [Variable]

If a static library must be created from the export symbol list to correctly link with a shared library, 'old_archive_from_expsyms_cmds' contains the commands needed to create that static library. When these commands are executed, the variable **soname** contains the name of the shared library in question, and the '$objdir/$newlib' contains the path of the static library these commands should build. After executing these commands, libtool will proceed to link against '$objdir/$newlib' instead of **soname**.

`lock_old_archive_extraction` [Variable]

Set to 'yes' if the extraction of a static library requires locking the library file. This is required on Darwin.

`build` [Variable]
`build_alias` [Variable]
`build_os` [Variable]

Set to the specified and canonical names of the system that libtool was built on.

`build_libtool_libs` [Variable]

Whether libtool should build shared libraries on this system. Set to 'yes' or 'no'.

`build_old_libs` [Variable]

Whether libtool should build static libraries on this system. Set to 'yes' or 'no'.

`compiler_c_o` [Variable]

Whether the compiler supports the -c and -o options simultaneously. Set to 'yes' or 'no'.

`compiler_needs_object` [Variable]

Whether the compiler has to see an object listed on the command line in order to successfully invoke the linker. If 'no', then a set of convenience archives or a set of object file names can be passed via linker-specific options or linker scripts.

`dlopen_support` [Variable]

Whether **dlopen** is supported on the platform. Set to 'yes' or 'no'.

`dlopen_self` [Variable]

Whether it is possible to **dlopen** the executable itself. Set to 'yes' or 'no'.

`dlopen_self_static` [Variable]

Whether it is possible to **dlopen** the executable itself, when it is linked statically (-all-static). Set to 'yes' or 'no'.

exclude_expsyms   [Variable]

> List of symbols that should not be listed in the preloaded symbols.

export_dynamic_flag_spec   [Variable]

> Compiler link flag that allows a dlopened shared library to reference symbols that are defined in the program.

export_symbols_cmds   [Variable]

> Commands to extract exported symbols from `libobjs` to the file `export_symbols`.

extract_expsyms_cmds   [Variable]

> Commands to extract the exported symbols list from a shared library. These commands are executed if there is no file '`$objdir/$soname-def`', and should write the names of the exported symbols to that file, for the use of '`old_archive_from_expsyms_cmds`'.

fast_install   [Variable]

> Determines whether libtool will privilege the installer or the developer. The assumption is that installers will seldom run programs in the build tree, and the developer will seldom install. This is only meaningful on platforms where `shlibpath_overrides_runpath` is not 'yes', so `fast_install` will be set to 'needless' in this case. If `fast_install` set to 'yes', libtool will create programs that search for installed libraries, and, if a program is run in the build tree, a new copy will be linked on-demand to use the yet-to-be-installed libraries. If set to 'no', libtool will create programs that use the yet-to-be-installed libraries, and will link a new copy of the program at install time. The default value is 'yes' or 'needless', depending on platform and configuration flags, and it can be turned from 'yes' to 'no' with the configure flag `--disable-fast-install`.
>
> On some systems, the linker always hardcodes paths to dependent libraries into the output. In this case, `fast_install` is never set to 'yes', and relinking at install time is triggered. This also means that `DESTDIR` installation does not work as expected.

file_magic_glob   [Variable]

> How to find potential files when `deplibs_check_method` is 'file_magic'. `file_magic_glob` is a `sed` expression, and the `sed` instance is fed potential file names that are transformed by the `file_magic_glob` expression. Useful when the shell does not support the shell option `nocaseglob`, making `want_nocaseglob` inappropriate. Normally disabled (i.e. `file_magic_glob` is empty).

finish_cmds   [Variable]

> Commands to tell the dynamic linker how to find shared libraries in a specific directory.

finish_eval   [Variable]

> Same as `finish_cmds`, except the commands are not displayed.

global_symbol_pipe   [Variable]

> A pipeline that takes the output of `NM`, and produces a listing of raw symbols followed by their C names. For example:

```
$ eval "$NM progname | $global_symbol_pipe"
D symbol1 C-symbol1
T symbol2 C-symbol2
C symbol3 C-symbol3
...
$
```

The first column contains the symbol type (used to tell data from code) but its meaning is system dependent.

global_symbol_to_cdecl   [Variable]

A pipeline that translates the output of `global_symbol_pipe` into proper C declarations. Since some platforms, such as HP/UX, have linkers that differentiate code from data, data symbols are declared as data, and code symbols are declared as functions.

hardcode_action   [Variable]

Either 'immediate' or 'relink', depending on whether shared library paths can be hardcoded into executables before they are installed, or if they need to be relinked.

hardcode_direct   [Variable]

Set to 'yes' or 'no', depending on whether the linker hardcodes directories if a library is directly specified on the command line (such as 'dir/libname.a') when `hardcode_libdir_flag_spec` is specified.

hardcode_direct_absolute   [Variable]

Some architectures hardcode "absolute" library directories that cannot be overridden by `shlibpath_var` when `hardcode_direct` is 'yes'. In that case set `hardcode_direct_absolute` to 'yes', or otherwise 'no'.

hardcode_into_libs   [Variable]

Whether the platform supports hardcoding of run-paths into libraries. If enabled, linking of programs will be much simpler but libraries will need to be relinked during installation. Set to 'yes' or 'no'.

hardcode_libdir_flag_spec   [Variable]

Flag to hardcode a `libdir` variable into a binary, so that the dynamic linker searches `libdir` for shared libraries at runtime. If it is empty, libtool will try to use some other hardcoding mechanism.

hardcode_libdir_separator   [Variable]

If the compiler only accepts a single `hardcode_libdir_flag`, then this variable contains the string that should separate multiple arguments to that flag.

hardcode_minus_L   [Variable]

Set to 'yes' or 'no', depending on whether the linker hardcodes directories specified by -L flags into the resulting executable when `hardcode_libdir_flag_spec` is specified.

hardcode_shlibpath_var   [Variable]

Set to 'yes' or 'no', depending on whether the linker hardcodes directories by writing the contents of '$shlibpath_var' into the resulting executable when `hardcode_libdir_flag_spec` is specified. Set to 'unsupported' if directories specified by '$shlibpath_var' are searched at run time, but not at link time.

host   [Variable]

host_alias   [Variable]

host_os   [Variable]

> Set to the specified and canonical names of the system that libtool was configured for.

include_expsyms   [Variable]

> List of symbols that must always be exported when using `export_symbols`.

inherit_rpath   [Variable]

> Whether the linker adds runtime paths of dependency libraries to the runtime path list, requiring libtool to relink the output when installing. Set to 'yes' or 'no'. Default is 'no'.

install_override_mode   [Variable]

> Permission mode override for installation of shared libraries. If the runtime linker fails to load libraries with wrong permissions, then it may fail to execute programs that are needed during installation, because these need the library that has just been installed. In this case, it is necessary to pass the mode to `install` with `-m install_override_mode`.

libext   [Variable]

> The standard old archive suffix (normally 'a').

libname_spec   [Variable]

> The format of a library name prefix. On all Unix systems, static libraries are called '`libname.a`', but on some systems (such as OS/2 or MS-DOS), the library is just called '`name.a`'.

library_names_spec   [Variable]

> A list of shared library names. The first is the name of the file, the rest are symbolic links to the file. The name in the list is the file name that the linker finds when given `-lname`.

link_all_deplibs   [Variable]

> Whether libtool must link a program against all its dependency libraries. Set to 'yes' or 'no'. Default is 'unknown', which is a synonym for 'yes'.

link_static_flag   [Variable]

> Linker flag (passed through the C compiler) used to prevent dynamic linking.

macro_version   [Variable]

macro_revision   [Variable]

> The release and revision from which the libtool.m4 macros were taken. This is used to ensure that macros and `ltmain.sh` correspond to the same Libtool version.

max_cmd_len   [Variable]

> The approximate longest command line that can be passed to '`$SHELL`' without being truncated, as computed by '`LT_CMD_MAX_LEN`'.

need_lib_prefix   [Variable]

> Whether we can dlopen modules without a 'lib' prefix. Set to 'yes' or 'no'. By default, it is 'unknown', which means the same as 'yes', but documents that we are not really sure about it. 'no' means that it is possible to dlopen a module without the 'lib' prefix.

need_version   [Variable]

> Whether versioning is required for libraries, i.e. whether the dynamic linker requires a version suffix for all libraries. Set to 'yes' or 'no'. By default, it is 'unknown', which means the same as 'yes', but documents that we are not really sure about it.

need_locks   [Variable]

> Whether files must be locked to prevent conflicts when compiling simultaneously. Set to 'yes' or 'no'.

nm_file_list_spec   [Variable]

> Specify filename containing input files for NM.

no_builtin_flag   [Variable]

> Compiler flag to disable builtin functions that conflict with declaring external global symbols as char.

no_undefined_flag   [Variable]

> The flag that is used by 'archive_cmds' to declare that there will be no unresolved symbols in the resulting shared library. Empty, if no such flag is required.

objdir   [Variable]

> The name of the directory that contains temporary libtool files.

objext   [Variable]

> The standard object file suffix (normally 'o').

pic_flag   [Variable]

> Any additional compiler flags for building library object files.

postinstall_cmds   [Variable]
old_postinstall_cmds   [Variable]

> Commands run after installing a shared or static library, respectively.

postuninstall_cmds   [Variable]
old_postuninstall_cmds   [Variable]

> Commands run after uninstalling a shared or static library, respectively.

postlink_cmds   [Variable]

> Commands necessary for finishing linking programs. postlink_cmds are executed immediately after the program is linked. Any occurrence of the string @OUTPUT@ in postlink_cmds is replaced by the name of the created executable (i.e. not the wrapper, if a wrapper is generated) prior to execution. Similarly, @TOOL_OUTPUT@ is replaced by the toolchain format of @OUTPUT@. Normally disabled (i.e. postlink_cmds empty).

reload_cmds   [Variable]
reload_flag   [Variable]
> Commands to create a reloadable object. Set `reload_cmds` to 'false' on systems that cannot create reloadable objects.

runpath_var   [Variable]
> The environment variable that tells the linker what directories to hardcode in the resulting executable.

shlibpath_overrides_runpath   [Variable]
> Indicates whether it is possible to override the hard-coded library search path of a program with an environment variable. If this is set to no, libtool may have to create two copies of a program in the build tree, one to be installed and one to be run in the build tree only. When each of these copies is created depends on the value of `fast_install`. The default value is 'unknown', which is equivalent to 'no'.

shlibpath_var   [Variable]
> The environment variable that tells the dynamic linker where to find shared libraries.

soname_spec   [Variable]
> The name coded into shared libraries, if different from the real name of the file.

striplib   [Variable]
old_striplib   [Variable]
> Command to strip a shared (`striplib`) or static (`old_striplib`) library, respectively. If these variables are empty, the strip flag in the install mode will be ignored for libraries (see Section 4.4 [Install mode], page 22).

sys_lib_dlsearch_path_spec   [Variable]
> Expression to get the run-time system library search path. Directories that appear in this list are never hard-coded into executables.

sys_lib_search_path_spec   [Variable]
> Expression to get the compile-time system library search path. This variable is used by libtool when it has to test whether a certain library is shared or static. The directories listed in `shlibpath_var` are automatically appended to this list, every time libtool runs (i.e., not at configuration time), because some linkers use this variable to extend the library search path. Linker switches such as -L also augment the search path.

thread_safe_flag_spec   [Variable]
> Linker flag (passed through the C compiler) used to generate thread-safe libraries.

to_host_file_cmd   [Variable]
> If the toolchain is not native to the build platform (e.g. if you are using MSYS to drive the scripting, but are using the MinGW native Windows compiler) this variable describes how to convert file names from the format used by the build platform to the format used by host platform. Normally set to 'func_convert_file_noop', libtool will autodetect most cases where other values should be used. On rare occasions, it may be necessary to override the autodetected value (see Section 15.3.7.6 [Cygwin to MinGW Cross], page 96).

to_tool_file_cmd   [Variable]

> If the toolchain is not native to the build platform (e.g. if you are using some Unix to drive the scripting together with a Windows toolchain running in Wine) this variable describes how to convert file names from the format used by the build platform to the format used by the toolchain. Normally set to '`func_convert_file_noop`'.

version_type   [Variable]

> The library version numbering type. One of '`libtool`', '`freebsd-aout`', '`freebsd-elf`', '`irix`', '`linux`', '`osf`', '`sunos`', '`windows`', or '`none`'.

want_nocaseglob   [Variable]

> Find potential files using the shell option `nocaseglob`, when `deplibs_check_method` is '`file_magic`'. Normally set to '`no`'. Set to '`yes`' to enable the `nocaseglob` shell option when looking for potential file names in a case-insensitive manner.

whole_archive_flag_spec   [Variable]

> Compiler flag to generate shared objects from convenience archives.

wl   [Variable]

> The C compiler flag that allows libtool to pass a flag directly to the linker. Used as: `${wl}`*some-flag*.

Variables ending in '`_cmds`' or '`_eval`' contain a '`~`'-separated list of commands that are `eval`ed one after another. If any of the commands return a nonzero exit status, libtool generally exits with an error message.

Variables ending in '`_spec`' are `eval`ed before being used by libtool.

15.5 Cheap tricks

Here are a few tricks that you can use to make maintainership easier:

- When people report bugs, ask them to use the `--config`, `--debug`, or `--features` flags, if you think they will help you. These flags are there to help you get information directly, rather than having to trust second-hand observation.

- Rather than reconfiguring libtool every time I make a change to `ltmain.in`, I keep a permanent `libtool` script in my `PATH`, which sources `ltmain.in` directly.

  The following steps describe how to create such a script, where `/home/src/libtool` is the directory containing the libtool source tree, `/home/src/libtool/libtool` is a libtool script that has been configured for your platform, and `~/bin` is a directory in your `PATH`:

```
trick$ cd ~/bin
trick$ sed 's%^\(macro_version=\).*$%\1@VERSION@%;
            s%^\(macro_revision=\).*$%\1@package_revision@%;
            /^# ltmain\.sh/q' /home/src/libtool/libtool > libtool
trick$ echo '. /home/src/libtool/ltmain.in' >> libtool
trick$ chmod +x libtool
trick$ libtool --version
ltmain.sh (GNU @PACKAGE@@TIMESTAMP@) @VERSION@

Copyright (C) 2014 Free Software Foundation, Inc.
This is free software; see the source for copying conditions.  There is NO
```

```
        warranty; not even for MERCHANTABILITY or FITNESS FOR A PARTICULAR PURPOSE.
        trick$
```

The output of the final 'libtool --version' command shows that the ltmain.in script is being used directly. Now, modify ~/bin/libtool or /home/src/libtool/ltmain.in directly in order to test new changes without having to rerun configure.

Appendix A GNU Free Documentation License

Version 1.3, 3 November 2008

Copyright © 2000, 2001, 2002, 2007, 2008 Free Software Foundation, Inc.
`http://fsf.org/`

Everyone is permitted to copy and distribute verbatim copies
of this license document, but changing it is not allowed.

0. PREAMBLE

The purpose of this License is to make a manual, textbook, or other functional and useful document *free* in the sense of freedom: to assure everyone the effective freedom to copy and redistribute it, with or without modifying it, either commercially or non-commercially. Secondarily, this License preserves for the author and publisher a way to get credit for their work, while not being considered responsible for modifications made by others.

This License is a kind of "copyleft", which means that derivative works of the document must themselves be free in the same sense. It complements the GNU General Public License, which is a copyleft license designed for free software.

We have designed this License in order to use it for manuals for free software, because free software needs free documentation: a free program should come with manuals providing the same freedoms that the software does. But this License is not limited to software manuals; it can be used for any textual work, regardless of subject matter or whether it is published as a printed book. We recommend this License principally for works whose purpose is instruction or reference.

1. APPLICABILITY AND DEFINITIONS

This License applies to any manual or other work, in any medium, that contains a notice placed by the copyright holder saying it can be distributed under the terms of this License. Such a notice grants a world-wide, royalty-free license, unlimited in duration, to use that work under the conditions stated herein. The "Document", below, refers to any such manual or work. Any member of the public is a licensee, and is addressed as "you". You accept the license if you copy, modify or distribute the work in a way requiring permission under copyright law.

A "Modified Version" of the Document means any work containing the Document or a portion of it, either copied verbatim, or with modifications and/or translated into another language.

A "Secondary Section" is a named appendix or a front-matter section of the Document that deals exclusively with the relationship of the publishers or authors of the Document to the Document's overall subject (or to related matters) and contains nothing that could fall directly within that overall subject. (Thus, if the Document is in part a textbook of mathematics, a Secondary Section may not explain any mathematics.) The relationship could be a matter of historical connection with the subject or with related matters, or of legal, commercial, philosophical, ethical or political position regarding them.

The "Invariant Sections" are certain Secondary Sections whose titles are designated, as being those of Invariant Sections, in the notice that says that the Document is released under this License. If a section does not fit the above definition of Secondary then it is not allowed to be designated as Invariant. The Document may contain zero Invariant Sections. If the Document does not identify any Invariant Sections then there are none.

The "Cover Texts" are certain short passages of text that are listed, as Front-Cover Texts or Back-Cover Texts, in the notice that says that the Document is released under this License. A Front-Cover Text may be at most 5 words, and a Back-Cover Text may be at most 25 words.

A "Transparent" copy of the Document means a machine-readable copy, represented in a format whose specification is available to the general public, that is suitable for revising the document straightforwardly with generic text editors or (for images composed of pixels) generic paint programs or (for drawings) some widely available drawing editor, and that is suitable for input to text formatters or for automatic translation to a variety of formats suitable for input to text formatters. A copy made in an otherwise Transparent file format whose markup, or absence of markup, has been arranged to thwart or discourage subsequent modification by readers is not Transparent. An image format is not Transparent if used for any substantial amount of text. A copy that is not "Transparent" is called "Opaque".

Examples of suitable formats for Transparent copies include plain ASCII without markup, Texinfo input format, LaTeX input format, SGML or XML using a publicly available DTD, and standard-conforming simple HTML, PostScript or PDF designed for human modification. Examples of transparent image formats include PNG, XCF and JPG. Opaque formats include proprietary formats that can be read and edited only by proprietary word processors, SGML or XML for which the DTD and/or processing tools are not generally available, and the machine-generated HTML, PostScript or PDF produced by some word processors for output purposes only.

The "Title Page" means, for a printed book, the title page itself, plus such following pages as are needed to hold, legibly, the material this License requires to appear in the title page. For works in formats which do not have any title page as such, "Title Page" means the text near the most prominent appearance of the work's title, preceding the beginning of the body of the text.

The "publisher" means any person or entity that distributes copies of the Document to the public.

A section "Entitled XYZ" means a named subunit of the Document whose title either is precisely XYZ or contains XYZ in parentheses following text that translates XYZ in another language. (Here XYZ stands for a specific section name mentioned below, such as "Acknowledgements", "Dedications", "Endorsements", or "History".) To "Preserve the Title" of such a section when you modify the Document means that it remains a section "Entitled XYZ" according to this definition.

The Document may include Warranty Disclaimers next to the notice which states that this License applies to the Document. These Warranty Disclaimers are considered to be included by reference in this License, but only as regards disclaiming warranties: any other implication that these Warranty Disclaimers may have is void and has no effect on the meaning of this License.

2. VERBATIM COPYING

You may copy and distribute the Document in any medium, either commercially or noncommercially, provided that this License, the copyright notices, and the license notice saying this License applies to the Document are reproduced in all copies, and that you add no other conditions whatsoever to those of this License. You may not use technical measures to obstruct or control the reading or further copying of the copies you make or distribute. However, you may accept compensation in exchange for copies. If you distribute a large enough number of copies you must also follow the conditions in section 3.

You may also lend copies, under the same conditions stated above, and you may publicly display copies.

3. COPYING IN QUANTITY

If you publish printed copies (or copies in media that commonly have printed covers) of the Document, numbering more than 100, and the Document's license notice requires Cover Texts, you must enclose the copies in covers that carry, clearly and legibly, all these Cover Texts: Front-Cover Texts on the front cover, and Back-Cover Texts on the back cover. Both covers must also clearly and legibly identify you as the publisher of these copies. The front cover must present the full title with all words of the title equally prominent and visible. You may add other material on the covers in addition. Copying with changes limited to the covers, as long as they preserve the title of the Document and satisfy these conditions, can be treated as verbatim copying in other respects.

If the required texts for either cover are too voluminous to fit legibly, you should put the first ones listed (as many as fit reasonably) on the actual cover, and continue the rest onto adjacent pages.

If you publish or distribute Opaque copies of the Document numbering more than 100, you must either include a machine-readable Transparent copy along with each Opaque copy, or state in or with each Opaque copy a computer-network location from which the general network-using public has access to download using public-standard network protocols a complete Transparent copy of the Document, free of added material. If you use the latter option, you must take reasonably prudent steps, when you begin distribution of Opaque copies in quantity, to ensure that this Transparent copy will remain thus accessible at the stated location until at least one year after the last time you distribute an Opaque copy (directly or through your agents or retailers) of that edition to the public.

It is requested, but not required, that you contact the authors of the Document well before redistributing any large number of copies, to give them a chance to provide you with an updated version of the Document.

4. MODIFICATIONS

You may copy and distribute a Modified Version of the Document under the conditions of sections 2 and 3 above, provided that you release the Modified Version under precisely this License, with the Modified Version filling the role of the Document, thus licensing distribution and modification of the Modified Version to whoever possesses a copy of it. In addition, you must do these things in the Modified Version:

A. Use in the Title Page (and on the covers, if any) a title distinct from that of the Document, and from those of previous versions (which should, if there were any, be listed in the History section of the Document). You may use the same title as a previous version if the original publisher of that version gives permission.

B. List on the Title Page, as authors, one or more persons or entities responsible for authorship of the modifications in the Modified Version, together with at least five of the principal authors of the Document (all of its principal authors, if it has fewer than five), unless they release you from this requirement.

C. State on the Title page the name of the publisher of the Modified Version, as the publisher.

D. Preserve all the copyright notices of the Document.

E. Add an appropriate copyright notice for your modifications adjacent to the other copyright notices.

F. Include, immediately after the copyright notices, a license notice giving the public permission to use the Modified Version under the terms of this License, in the form shown in the Addendum below.

G. Preserve in that license notice the full lists of Invariant Sections and required Cover Texts given in the Document's license notice.

H. Include an unaltered copy of this License.

I. Preserve the section Entitled "History", Preserve its Title, and add to it an item stating at least the title, year, new authors, and publisher of the Modified Version as given on the Title Page. If there is no section Entitled "History" in the Document, create one stating the title, year, authors, and publisher of the Document as given on its Title Page, then add an item describing the Modified Version as stated in the previous sentence.

J. Preserve the network location, if any, given in the Document for public access to a Transparent copy of the Document, and likewise the network locations given in the Document for previous versions it was based on. These may be placed in the "History" section. You may omit a network location for a work that was published at least four years before the Document itself, or if the original publisher of the version it refers to gives permission.

K. For any section Entitled "Acknowledgements" or "Dedications", Preserve the Title of the section, and preserve in the section all the substance and tone of each of the contributor acknowledgements and/or dedications given therein.

L. Preserve all the Invariant Sections of the Document, unaltered in their text and in their titles. Section numbers or the equivalent are not considered part of the section titles.

M. Delete any section Entitled "Endorsements". Such a section may not be included in the Modified Version.

N. Do not retitle any existing section to be Entitled "Endorsements" or to conflict in title with any Invariant Section.

O. Preserve any Warranty Disclaimers.

If the Modified Version includes new front-matter sections or appendices that qualify as Secondary Sections and contain no material copied from the Document, you may at your option designate some or all of these sections as invariant. To do this, add their titles to the list of Invariant Sections in the Modified Version's license notice. These titles must be distinct from any other section titles.

You may add a section Entitled "Endorsements", provided it contains nothing but endorsements of your Modified Version by various parties—for example, statements of peer review or that the text has been approved by an organization as the authoritative definition of a standard.

You may add a passage of up to five words as a Front-Cover Text, and a passage of up to 25 words as a Back-Cover Text, to the end of the list of Cover Texts in the Modified Version. Only one passage of Front-Cover Text and one of Back-Cover Text may be added by (or through arrangements made by) any one entity. If the Document already includes a cover text for the same cover, previously added by you or by arrangement made by the same entity you are acting on behalf of, you may not add another; but you may replace the old one, on explicit permission from the previous publisher that added the old one.

The author(s) and publisher(s) of the Document do not by this License give permission to use their names for publicity for or to assert or imply endorsement of any Modified Version.

5. COMBINING DOCUMENTS

You may combine the Document with other documents released under this License, under the terms defined in section 4 above for modified versions, provided that you include in the combination all of the Invariant Sections of all of the original documents, unmodified, and list them all as Invariant Sections of your combined work in its license notice, and that you preserve all their Warranty Disclaimers.

The combined work need only contain one copy of this License, and multiple identical Invariant Sections may be replaced with a single copy. If there are multiple Invariant Sections with the same name but different contents, make the title of each such section unique by adding at the end of it, in parentheses, the name of the original author or publisher of that section if known, or else a unique number. Make the same adjustment to the section titles in the list of Invariant Sections in the license notice of the combined work.

In the combination, you must combine any sections Entitled "History" in the various original documents, forming one section Entitled "History"; likewise combine any sections Entitled "Acknowledgements", and any sections Entitled "Dedications". You must delete all sections Entitled "Endorsements."

6. COLLECTIONS OF DOCUMENTS

You may make a collection consisting of the Document and other documents released under this License, and replace the individual copies of this License in the various documents with a single copy that is included in the collection, provided that you follow the rules of this License for verbatim copying of each of the documents in all other respects.

You may extract a single document from such a collection, and distribute it individually under this License, provided you insert a copy of this License into the extracted document, and follow this License in all other respects regarding verbatim copying of that document.

7. AGGREGATION WITH INDEPENDENT WORKS

A compilation of the Document or its derivatives with other separate and independent documents or works, in or on a volume of a storage or distribution medium, is called an "aggregate" if the copyright resulting from the compilation is not used to limit the legal rights of the compilation's users beyond what the individual works permit. When the Document is included in an aggregate, this License does not apply to the other works in the aggregate which are not themselves derivative works of the Document.

If the Cover Text requirement of section 3 is applicable to these copies of the Document, then if the Document is less than one half of the entire aggregate, the Document's Cover Texts may be placed on covers that bracket the Document within the aggregate, or the electronic equivalent of covers if the Document is in electronic form. Otherwise they must appear on printed covers that bracket the whole aggregate.

8. TRANSLATION

Translation is considered a kind of modification, so you may distribute translations of the Document under the terms of section 4. Replacing Invariant Sections with translations requires special permission from their copyright holders, but you may include translations of some or all Invariant Sections in addition to the original versions of these Invariant Sections. You may include a translation of this License, and all the license notices in the Document, and any Warranty Disclaimers, provided that you also include the original English version of this License and the original versions of those notices and disclaimers. In case of a disagreement between the translation and the original version of this License or a notice or disclaimer, the original version will prevail.

If a section in the Document is Entitled "Acknowledgements", "Dedications", or "History", the requirement (section 4) to Preserve its Title (section 1) will typically require changing the actual title.

9. TERMINATION

You may not copy, modify, sublicense, or distribute the Document except as expressly provided under this License. Any attempt otherwise to copy, modify, sublicense, or distribute it is void, and will automatically terminate your rights under this License.

However, if you cease all violation of this License, then your license from a particular copyright holder is reinstated (a) provisionally, unless and until the copyright holder explicitly and finally terminates your license, and (b) permanently, if the copyright holder fails to notify you of the violation by some reasonable means prior to 60 days after the cessation.

Moreover, your license from a particular copyright holder is reinstated permanently if the copyright holder notifies you of the violation by some reasonable means, this is the first time you have received notice of violation of this License (for any work) from that copyright holder, and you cure the violation prior to 30 days after your receipt of the notice.

Termination of your rights under this section does not terminate the licenses of parties who have received copies or rights from you under this License. If your rights have been terminated and not permanently reinstated, receipt of a copy of some or all of the same material does not give you any rights to use it.

10. FUTURE REVISIONS OF THIS LICENSE

The Free Software Foundation may publish new, revised versions of the GNU Free Documentation License from time to time. Such new versions will be similar in spirit to the present version, but may differ in detail to address new problems or concerns. See `http://www.gnu.org/copyleft/`.

Each version of the License is given a distinguishing version number. If the Document specifies that a particular numbered version of this License "or any later version" applies to it, you have the option of following the terms and conditions either of that specified version or of any later version that has been published (not as a draft) by the Free Software Foundation. If the Document does not specify a version number of this License, you may choose any version ever published (not as a draft) by the Free Software Foundation. If the Document specifies that a proxy can decide which future versions of this License can be used, that proxy's public statement of acceptance of a version permanently authorizes you to choose that version for the Document.

11. RELICENSING

"Massive Multiauthor Collaboration Site" (or "MMC Site") means any World Wide Web server that publishes copyrightable works and also provides prominent facilities for anybody to edit those works. A public wiki that anybody can edit is an example of such a server. A "Massive Multiauthor Collaboration" (or "MMC") contained in the site means any set of copyrightable works thus published on the MMC site.

"CC-BY-SA" means the Creative Commons Attribution-Share Alike 3.0 license published by Creative Commons Corporation, a not-for-profit corporation with a principal place of business in San Francisco, California, as well as future copyleft versions of that license published by that same organization.

"Incorporate" means to publish or republish a Document, in whole or in part, as part of another Document.

An MMC is "eligible for relicensing" if it is licensed under this License, and if all works that were first published under this License somewhere other than this MMC, and subsequently incorporated in whole or in part into the MMC, (1) had no cover texts or invariant sections, and (2) were thus incorporated prior to November 1, 2008.

The operator of an MMC Site may republish an MMC contained in the site under CC-BY-SA on the same site at any time before August 1, 2009, provided the MMC is eligible for relicensing.

ADDENDUM: How to use this License for your documents

To use this License in a document you have written, include a copy of the License in the document and put the following copyright and license notices just after the title page:

```
Copyright (C)  year  your name.
Permission is granted to copy, distribute and/or modify this document
under the terms of the GNU Free Documentation License, Version 1.3
or any later version published by the Free Software Foundation;
with no Invariant Sections, no Front-Cover Texts, and no Back-Cover
Texts.  A copy of the license is included in the section entitled ''GNU
Free Documentation License''.
```

If you have Invariant Sections, Front-Cover Texts and Back-Cover Texts, replace the "with...Texts." line with this:

```
with the Invariant Sections being list their titles, with
the Front-Cover Texts being list, and with the Back-Cover Texts
being list.
```

If you have Invariant Sections without Cover Texts, or some other combination of the three, merge those two alternatives to suit the situation.

If your document contains nontrivial examples of program code, we recommend releasing these examples in parallel under your choice of free software license, such as the GNU General Public License, to permit their use in free software.

Combined Index   118

Combined Index

M

N

O